P9-EDT-814

JOE FAFARD

THE BRONZE YEARS

THE MONTREAL MUSEUM
OF FINE ARTS

The exhibition *Joe Fafard: The Bronze Years*, organized by Pierre Théberge, Director, was shown at the Montreal Museum of Fine Arts from November 21, 1996, to February 16, 1997.

The exhibition was curated and the catalogue edited by Mayo Graham, Chief Curator.

This catalogue is a production of the Publications Department, Communications Division, the Montreal Museum of Fine Arts

Production co-ordination: Denise L. Bissonnette
Revision : Donald Pistolesi
Photographs of the works: see p. 119
Graphic design and typesetting : France Lafond design graphique
Photo-engraving and printing: Richard Veilleux imprimeur

All rights reserved.
The reproduction of any part of this book without the prior consent of the publisher is an infringement of the Copyright Act, Chapter C-42, R.S.C., 1985.

© The Montreal Museum of Fine Arts, 1996
Reproductions of the works
© Joe Fafard, 1996

ISBN: 2-89192-217-4

Legal deposit - 4th trimester 1996
Bibliothèque nationale du Québec
National Library of Canada

THE MONTREAL MUSEUM OF FINE ARTS
P.O. Box 3000, Station "H"
Montreal, Quebec H3G 2T9

PRINTED IN CANADA

AUGUSTANA LIBRARY
UNIVERSITY OF ALBERTA

Contents

Preface	5
Pierre Théberge	
Introduction	7
Mayo Graham	
Joe Fafard: An Essay in Three Parts	11
Asleep in His Mother's House	12
The Pasture	24
Dear Vincent	29
Nancy Tousley	
Exhibited Works	
Artists and Other Figures (Nos. 1-33)	33
Cattle and Horses (Nos. 34-76)	59
Tables (Nos. 77-88)	91
Cattle and Horses in Stainless Steel (Nos. 89-108)	101
The Artist's Techniques	107
Mayo Graham	
Biographical Note	113
Solo Exhibitions	114
Selected Group Exhibitions	115
Selected Bibliography	116
Lenders to the Exhibition	117
List of Exhibited Works	118

The Fédération des producteurs de lait du Québec is proud to be associated with the Montreal Museum of Fine Arts for the presentation of the exhibition *Joe Fafard: The Bronze Years.*

One of those rare contemporary artists who is admired by both critics and the public, Joe Fafard grew up in rural Saskatchewan; and it is from his childhood surroundings that he derives inspiration for his bronze sculptures of farm animals. It is perhaps not purely a coincidence that the school where Fafard earned his Master of Fine Arts, the Pennsylvania State University, was, more than 130 years ago, the first institution of higher learning in the United States to award a degree in agricultural science.

This unique exhibition gives visitors an opportunity to admire, among other works, *The Pasture*, a group of seven larger-than-life bronze cows that will leave no one unmoved.

For a number of years, the Fédération des producteurs de lait has sought to lend its support to events offering original cultural programming to a broad public. This refreshing exhibition corresponds to the same high standards we aim for in the products we offer the public.

Quebec's 11,500 dairy producers hope that *Joe Fafard: The Bronze Years* will meet with resounding success.

Claude Rivard
President

Fédération
des producteurs
de lait du Québec

Preface

The sculptures of Joe Fafard, particularly well known in Western Canada, have captured the imagination of both artists and the public for many years. Although his work is not often seen beyond his Saskatchewan sod, three early Fafard plaster figures were included twenty-six years ago in *Survey/Sondage 70: Realism(e)s* at the Montreal Museum of Fine Arts.

Fafard's sculptures deserve to be much more widely known, and we are pleased to have this opportunity to present his work from the 1980s and 1990s, focussing on the bronzes. His exceptional ability to capture the essence of character and explore spatial language is always marked by wit and perspicacity.

The artist has worked closely with the curator of the exhibition, Mayo Graham, Chief Curator of the Montreal Museum of Fine Arts. They have known one another for some eighteen years, and the exhibition bears witness to an empathetic collaboration. Joe Fafard has been particularly generous with his time and interest in working on this project, and we are most grateful to him.

As well as texts by the curator, the catalogue benefits from an eminently readable three-part essay by Calgary writer and freelance curator Nancy Tousley.

We would like to thank the many lenders to the exhibition, who have most graciously agreed to part with their very special works for this exhibition. Without the exceedingly generous co-operation of these individuals, public institutions and corporations, our undertaking would not have been possible.

We are grateful to the Canada Council for its contribution towards this project. At the same time, we should like to acknowledge the generous support of the Quebec Ministère de la Culture et des Communications and the contribution of the Conseil des arts de la Communauté urbaine de Montréal towards the realization of this exhibition, among the many activities in our Museum they sustain.

And finally, we would like to acknowledge the assistance of Quebec's dairy association, the Fédération des producteurs de lait, who are the exhibition's main sponsor. Their support and that of our loyal partner the newspaper *La Presse* make possible the effective promotion of this exhibition to the public.

It is our hope that the creations of *Joe Fafard: The Bronze Years* will inspire inquiry, sustenance and joy.

Pierre Théberge, C.Q.
Director
The Montreal Museum of Fine Arts

Introduction

In 1992, Pierre Théberge invited Joe Fafard to visit the newly expanded Montreal Museum of Fine Arts and to discuss the idea of an exhibition. Fafard's French-Canadian heritage and the museum itself attracted him to the idea of a major Montreal exhibition. Known at first for his diminutive ceramic sculptures of people and cows, by late 1985 Fafard was working primarily in bronze, often on a large scale. The present exhibition focusses on the past dozen years, during which Fafard found a special aptitude for this medium.

Three thematic threads wind through the exhibition: artists, cattle and horses, and tables. The artist-related sculptures show Fafard's ability to capture the essence of character and his fundamental interest in certain artists, such as Picasso, Van Gogh and Cézanne, and their art. Several large heads and other earlier works in clay provide a point of reference to the more recent bronzes. Different versions of several pieces have been included to illuminate Fafard's continuing exploration of mediums and ways of treating them, as well as his handling of colour – in glaze, paint and patina. Also included with this artist group are a few allegorical-archetypal figures, like *Manitoba* (cat. 27), *Cortez* (cat. 31) and *Joan of Arc* (cat. 32).

Domestic animals have populated Fafard's landscape from his earliest childhood. His bronze cows, bulls, calves and more recent horses provide the basis for an investigation of form. Their familiar shapes are flattened, truncated or reduced to essential outline as Fafard works to animate space while providing the illusion of volume. In the last several years, the artist has used laser-cut steel to further collapse the third dimension.

The third group of sculptural work in the exhibition – a number of tables (and a chair) – provides a concentrated moment to examine Fafard's wit, which, whether playful, joyful, erotic or caustic, is an essential condition of his work. The tables first

Fig. 1. Mongolia, *Ornamental Plaque*,
4th-3rd c. B.C., bronze, 4.5 x 10.8 cm
The Montreal Museum of Fine Arts, 1931.Dm.5

Fig. 2. Maurice Cullen, *Bull in Pasture*, 1919, oil on canvas, 46 x 55.5 cm
The Montreal Museum of Fine Arts, 1960.724

took shape as experiments in sand-casting bronze. They grew into narratives with more complex themes and spatial organization.

The creative artist and the domestic animal both have a long and noble history as subjects in art. Among portraits of artists by other artists, one thinks of Van Dyck's series of etchings of poets and painters of his day, Fantin-Latour's group portraits of artists and writers, or Rodin's *Balzac*. Animal subjects are the continuation of a tradition that runs from the murals of prehistoric cave dwellers, Egyptian chronicles in stone and two-thousand-year-old Mongolian bronze plaques (fig. 1) to Degas's bronze horses and Maurice Cullen's *Bull in Pasture* (fig. 2). The incorporation of bronze animal figures into decorative objects finds precedents from ancient Rome to the nineteenth-century candelabras of Barye,[1] and for furniture, in Diego Giacometti's fanciful tables and chairs.

Fig. 3. *My Picasso*, 1981 (cat. 19)

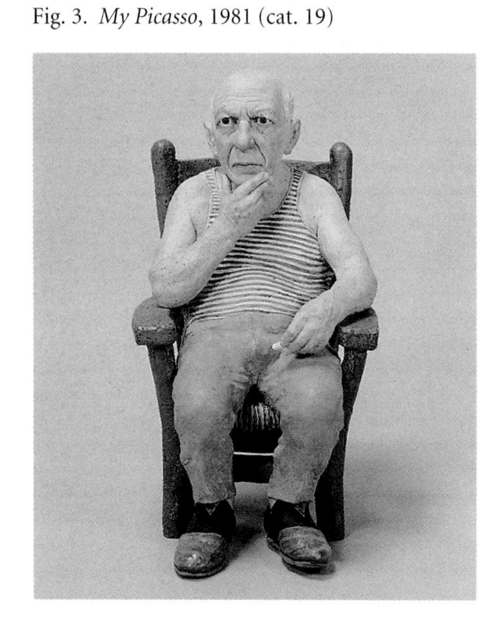

The first artists Fafard portrayed were Picasso (fig. 3), Matisse and Cézanne. The large clay head of Cézanne in the collection of the National Gallery of Canada (cat. 13) dates from 1981. The series of forty ceramic "self-portraits" of Van Gogh (cat. 8) extended from 1982 to 1987. *Dear Vincent* (cat. 2), the first bronze, was test cast in 1984. Fafard has said that these artists "are mythic figures in my mind . . . I'm not trying to place myself within this or that tradition when I do a portrait of van Gogh. I see myself rather as paying homage to this particular guy, who was the originator of this marvelous work."[2] Referring to the landscape he painted on the back of a large head of Cézanne, Fafard has said that it has "to do with Cézanne's work in terms of the flattening and raising up of the landscape in the picture plane. What I was working with at the time seemed to lend itself very well to that. As well, of course I'm a longtime admirer of Cézanne's painting."[3]

The flattening of form, the reduction of sculpture's third dimension, started with a piece Fafard produced in late 1980 for an invitational exhibition organized by the Campbell Museum, of Camden, New Jersey, in honour of the two-hundred-and-fiftieth anniversary of the birth of Josiah Wedgwood. Fafard chose to create a portrait bust of Queen Elizabeth II, inasmuch as Wedgwood "always did things for kings and queens". Fafard made the portrait as a flat profile, "taking her face off a penny. I did both sides, both flat, with one in reverse . . . I made her kind of like a

1. With such ornate titles as "Twelve-light Candelabra with Fruits, Leaves and Roots of the Poppy, a Serpent about the Stem and Surmounted by a Bird".

2. Interview in Matthew Teitelbaum and Peter White, *Joe Fafard: Cows and Other Luminaries, 1977-1987*, exhib. cat. (Saskatoon: Mendel Art Gallery, 1987) p. 53.

3. From here on, the artist is quoted from an interview with the author that took place on November 11, 1995.

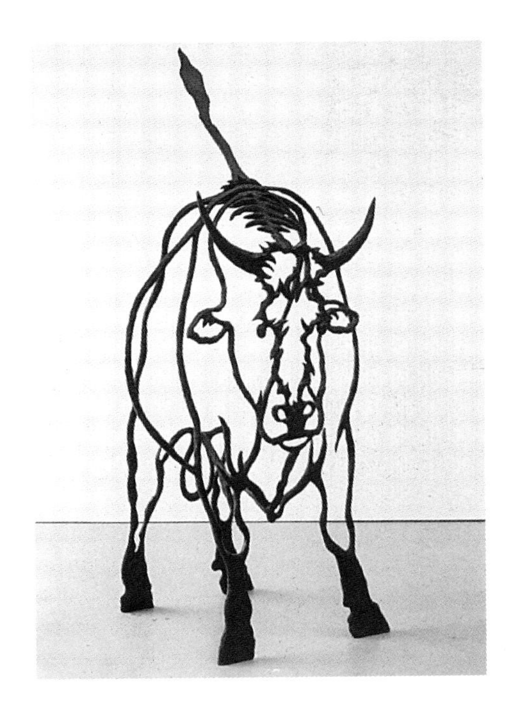

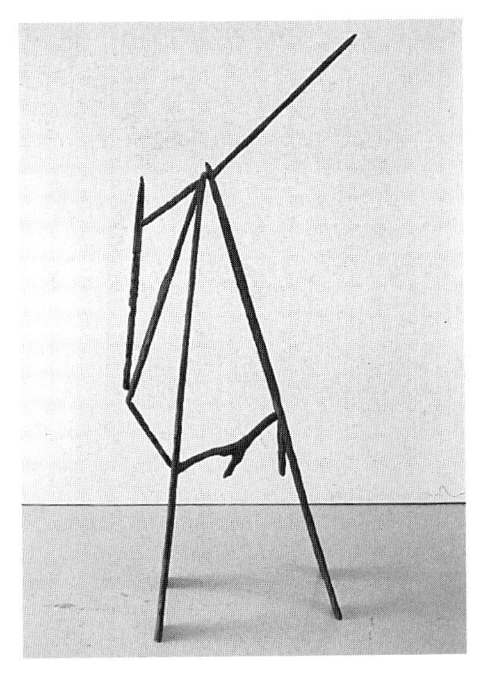

Fig. 4. *Gris*, 1991, front view (cat. 54)

Fig. 5. *Gris*, 1991, side view (cat. 54)

ship of state, presented on a cushion . . . When I turned the figure around, I thought of Alberto Giacometti. That's what got me started on the flat work. After that, I experimented with the cows." The first experiments were flat, in profile, but Fafard felt this was too close to Egyptian relief and that it didn't go far enough. Next, exploiting the malleability of clay, he flattened one of his cows from nose to tail. Starting in the late eighties, the properties of bronze, such as the tensile strength permitting holding lines in space, led him to further experimentation. Seen from the front, *Gris* (fig. 4) is very clearly an angry bull, albeit drawn in space. From the side (fig. 5), it appears as a few oblique lines, a sort of abstract tripod.

The linear characteristics of works such as *Gris* and *Zeta* (cat. 63) bear close connections to the table bases that Fafard began to create in 1986, following earlier table-like works that were rather bronze sculptures with integral bases. *Morris* (fig. 6) portrays a stolid, pot-bellied ape roosting in the swags of the table-leg branches, surmounted by a utilitarian glass top.[4] The undersize managers in the *Boxer Table* (cat. 78) and the naked rider of the *Explorer Table* (cat. 86) make pointed and humorous observations.

It seems clear that Fafard enjoys his work, just as Renoir did. "Renoir himself always seemed like an interesting character . . . I think back to that comment he was supposed to have made in art school, when his professor attacked him for being there just to amuse himself, and he thought, 'Why else would I be here?'"

M. G.

Fig. 6. *Morris*, 1987 (cat. 79)

4. At the time that this piece was created, Fafard was disputing the future of the MacKenzie Art Gallery with Morris Shumiatcher, a high-profile Regina lawyer.

Joe Fafard
An Essay in Three Parts

by Nancy Tousley

On the farm we grew wheat, oats, sometimes barley, occasionally flax, and beef and pork, and nearly all the family food, from potatoes to turnips to corn. Most of this food was consumed right on the farm. We used to can all the chicken for winter, and salt the pork, freeze the beef, or can it, but we would have to rely on freezing from the weather, not from refrigeration. We lived in a house made of logs that was not much bigger than my sunken living room. It had a second floor, which was the sleeping floor; it would be called a half-storey today because the walls were slanted. So, the farm was more or less a self-sufficient thing. There was very little cash economy. We got cash from the cream and we sold grain and we sold beef, but we didn't sell much pork because we mostly consumed it ourselves. We sold eggs. We went to town to buy things we couldn't grow on the farm, like sugar and salt and pepper and condiments, not much else. We'd buy flour. But it wasn't like you had to go to town much, you'd just go down to the basement to get your food. By fall the basement would be stuffed with the winter's food. Cabbages would be hanging upside down from the rafters, potatoes would be in a big bin, the walls would be lined with shelves that were loaded with canned food, like pork, poultry, beets, corn, and all those things. There was a lot of canned fruit because we picked wild fruit and we bought some fruit as well, from Ontario and British Columbia, like crabapples, pears and peaches, which we canned so that we had dessert. And underneath the stairs there was always a barrel or box of fresh apples and a barrel of salt pork. So when it came time to make dinner, my mother would always send one of us down to the basement to get potatoes, maybe a block of salt pork, a can of peaches. She'd send us shopping downstairs.[1]

1. Passages quoting Joe Fafard have been taken from interviews with this writer recorded at various times since 1987. For an earlier version of ideas developed here, see Nancy Tousley, "Community Spirit", *Canadian Art*, vol. 5, no. 1 (Spring 1988), pp. 56-61.

Asleep in His Mother's House

Early in his career, Joe Fafard made a ceramic wall plaque he called *Ma naissance* (fig. 1) as the starting point of a series of works about his childhood. Where better to begin? The only souvenir of the series that he has kept, the piece is a colourfully glazed low-relief "picture" of a farm spread out under a pale blue firmament capped by an arc of lavender clouds, with a fat yellow sun ascending behind it. In the distance, smoke rises from the chimney of a white house next to a red barn, while in the foreground, a burgeoning crop of russet potatoes presses forward as though, in its abundance, it were ready to spill out of the patch and onto the floor at a viewer's feet. Built up in certain parts into two and three dimensions, the "picture" gives depth and perspective to the halcyon scene. It is a metaphorical image: a vision of the agricultural landscape as an overflowing cornucopia.

In it, there is just one human figure. Gigantic within the miniature depicted world, a purple-faced newborn is emerging from the side of a yellow-green mound in the barnyard, as though the farm itself were the womb from which he comes sliding into the world, showing no signs of trauma. The representation of this miraculous event makes *Ma naissance* also an allegory: the story of the birth of the artist into an arcadian world imagined from the point of view of a child. Encircled by a green ruff of new leaves, the baby's peaceful face is rapt with dreaming, as though he has yet to awaken from a deep reverie. In the meantime, a herd of tiny cows makes its way across the top of the mound to take the sun, unaware that anything out of the ordinary is happening.

Created in 1971, *Ma naissance* began an autobiographical series that the artist projected to include about a dozen plaques in all but never completed. Fafard based their vignettes on episodes from his intensely remembered childhood. The series followed his life from birth to age eight or nine and then ran out of steam. By the time he made these works at the age of twenty-nine, Fafard had been away to school, seen a glimpse of the New York art world and returned to Saskatchewan.[2] He was searching for the place where human values might reside in art, his art, and going back to his beginnings. In many ways, he was reinventing himself even as he was reclaiming his identity.

More than once, Fafard has said that his perceptions of the world were shaped on the farm surrounding the village of Sainte-Marthe, Saskatchewan, near the Manitoba border. He was born and grew up there in a Catholic French-Canadian family, the sixth of twelve children, dwelling in a cultural enclave of French-Canadian and Métis families. His freely offered statement about his perceptions has most often been ignored, however, or if not ignored altogether, considered only to account for the farmyard animals in his sculptural repertoire. But what else could the shaping of the artist's perceptions on a farm in a tiny French-Canadian village

2. After he completed a Master of Fine Arts degree at Pennsylvania State University in 1968, Fafard returned to Saskatchewan and took a job as an instructor in sculpture at the University of Saskatchewan, Regina Campus. David Gilhooly, the American ceramic artist who based his work on the invention of a Frog World and was a graduate student of Robert Arneson's at the University of California, Davis, was also teaching at the Regina university at the time, from 1969-1974. Gilhooly's influence on Fafard, which was to grant him permission to seek the content of his art in his personal life and to validate play as a vital aspect of artmaking, has been well documented. See Matthew Teitelbaum and Peter White, *Joe Fafard: Cows and Other Luminaries, 1977-1987* (Saskatoon: Mendel Art Gallery, 1987), pp. 10-11, 47-49.

Fig. 1. Joe Fafard, *Ma naissance*, 1971, ceramic, diam: approx. 40 cm
Collection of the artist (See colour reproduction, front flap.)

mean, if, as they must be, "perceptions" are taken to encompass meanings, emotions, concepts and attitudes?

"Expose a child to a particular environment at his susceptible time and he will perceive in the shapes of that environment until he dies," writes Wallace Stegner in *Wolf Willow: A History, a Story and a Memory of the Last Plains Frontier*. "The perceptive habits that are like imprintings or like conditioned responses carry their habitual and remembered emotions."[3] The American writer, who grew up in Saskatchewan, is often quoted by Prairie writers mulling over the subjects of regional identity and voice, which he approached by intermingling history, fiction and autobiography. Implicit in Stegner's observations is the notion that the shapes of the environment include the culture and language of the social environment as well as the landscape and atmosphere of the natural environment. Language and culture are the screens that process the data, filter it and give it sense. How an individual perceives the world, be it the natural world or the social world, is a process mediated by culture.

In its isolation, Fafard's family created and cultivated its own history, and maintained its ties to the relations in Quebec through the use of narrative forms – storytelling and letter writing – that were part of everyday life. Fafard heard the story of his birth many times while he was growing up, as well as the tales of other dramatic childhood events, such as the story about the dark winter night when his mother Julienne struggled through a storm to get her ailing young son, suffering from appendicitis, to a doctor in town. The inspirations for the series of ceramic plaques were contained in stories like these, the episodes from Fafard's childhood that stood out in his memory as significant events.

They were like Stations of the Cross, these plaques, commemorating different events in my life. When I started working I worked a little bit autobiographically. I was making a little bit of fun, too, like the anecdotal stories we used to tell in my family. We come from the oral tradition and we always told stories in the family. So there would

3. Wallace Stegner, *Wolf Willow: A History, a Story and a Memory of the Last Plains Frontier* (Toronto: Macmillan of Canada, 1977), p. 21. This book was first published in 1955.

Fig. 2. Joe Fafard, *Mon père*, 1972, clay, h: 34 cm. Collection of the artist.

Fig. 3. Joe Fafard, *Ma mère*, 1972, clay, h: 28 cm. Collection of the artist.

always be some story attached to every member of the family and one of the stories attached to me was that I was a very difficult birth for my mother. But it came at a time when they were digging potatoes in the rain, because there was so much rain they had to get the potatoes out of the ground. It was September and it was flooding and it was the biggest potato crop there had ever been. So this [Ma naissance], *in my mind, was connected to digging potatoes out of the ground and to me coming from somewhere. I was a kid and, when you're a kid, they don't tell you where. So I made this plaque of the potatoes coming out of the ground and myself, as well, coming out of the side of the plaque, looking like a potato on purpose. The plaque is a fairly accurate description of the way the house was and the barn was, and the barnyard. Where I am coming out of the ground is where the manure pile was.*

The allegory of *Ma naissance* is not simply a story about the birth of Joe Fafard, however: it can be read on another level of meaning as an allegory of Fafard's birth *as* an artist. In the choice of setting and point of view, *Ma naissance* stands as a declaration of values and a point of origin for all the works that follow. The fertility of the farm, the dreaming newborn, the child's point of view, the embodiment of a story by a figure, and the use of the miniature and the gigantic, devices both of narrative and of visual art, point to telling principles that underlie the artist's work and recur in the content and form of his later oeuvre.

The declaration of values speaks first of the personal and the popular. Fafard experienced the time he spent as a student in the United States as an uprooting. When he went back home to Saskatchewan, he sought to recapture the sensorially rich, self-sufficient world he had left. His desire was to address human concerns in a way that could be easily understood by the man in the street. The art world of the time had no respect for ordinary working people, he believed, and the museums were temples that whispered they were "not for people like your father, Joe".[4] Even more fundamental was the question of voice: Stegner's compelling argument, which was not lost on the Saskatchewan writers who were Fafard's close friends in the early 1970s, had a double meaning for an artist working on the Prairies who was also a French Canadian. "Contradictory voices tell you who you are," Stegner writes. "You grow up speaking one dialect and reading and writing another . . . you may learn to be nimble in the King's English; yet in moments of relaxation, crisis, or surprise you fall back into the corrupted lingo of your native tongue. Nevertheless all the forces of culture and snobbery are against you *writing* by ear and making contact with your natural audience . . . You grow out of touch with your dialect because learning and literature lead you another way unless you consciously resist."[5]

Thus, the world that Fafard first set about to invoke through his work was the world of his childhood. That he chose to build it not on a loosely defined notion of the Prairies but on the French-Canadian culture of Sainte-Marthe can be inferred from the language of the title of that first autobiographical plaque: not *My Birth*, but *Ma naissance*. By using the French, he was declaring descent, a lineage and his roots in a specific place. "The readiest account of place might define it as the nation," writes Edward Said. "But this idea of place does not cover the nuances, principally of reassurance, fitness, belonging, association, and community, entailed in the phrase *at home* or *in place* . . . It is in culture that we can seek out the range of meanings and ideas conveyed by the phrases *belonging to* or *in a place*, being *at home in a place*."[6]

4. Léo Fafard died in 1972.

5. Stegner 1977, pp. 25-26. Using his own experience, Stegner was remarking on the struggle of the American writer to find an authentic voice for the American experience at a time when European art and culture were seen to be superior. Fafard did not read *Wolf Willow* until the 1980s, although he heard the talk going on around it within his circle of friends. In Saskatchewan, Stegner's work became a touchstone in discussions of regionalism and the development of a regional voice. The work that affected Fafard in the early 1970s, when he returned from New York, was the Sinclair Ross novel *As for Me and My House* (1941), the bleak Depression-era story of a minister and frustrated artist who struggles with isolation and alienation in the ironically named town of Horizon, Saskatchewan.

6. Edward Said, *The World, the Text, and the Critic* (Cambridge, Massachusetts: Havard University Press, 1983), p. 8.

Fig. 4. Philippe, Bernard, Lucille, Claude, Guy, cousin Donald and Joe at Sainte-Marthe, about 1946

Perhaps the red herring was the work that Fafard was making only two years later, in 1973, when he became widely known almost overnight as the subject of a National Film Board production, *I Don't Have to Work That Big*, which was broadcast that spring on CBC-TV. At the time, he was living in Pense, a hamlet of fewer than five hundred residents just outside of Regina.[7] As the newcomer to town, Fafard was embarked on the project of making small full-figure clay portraits of the townspeople. This interaction with the community was, in part, his way of getting to know people and learning the town's history. Around each of these clay portrait figures, there is a story, which is something that holds true for most of Fafard's work in clay and in bronze. Seen across the country on television, the "people of Pense", as this series of sculptures became known in the media, identified Fafard with generic small town Saskatchewan.[8] Yet these figures also emerge from the theme of origins as well as from Fafard's biography. Two of his earliest clay figures, both made in 1972, are of the primary contributors to this portrait of the artist that Fafard was building of himself – *Mon père* (Léo Fafard, fig. 2) and *Ma mère* (née Julienne Cantin, fig. 3), the Adam and Eve of Sainte-Marthe, who grew up there, were schoolmates, became childhood sweethearts, married there and made their family (fig. 4).

Fafard is the twelfth-generation offspring of a family that has direct ties to both France and French Canada and, on his father's side, has lived in Canada since the seventeenth century. The Fafards came from the village of Hotot, now a part of the town of Évreux, south of Rouen, in Normandy. Bertrand Fafard made the journey to New France by 1637, for his presence was recorded on the register of January 24, 1638. He acquired his first land holdings in the following year and, on December 21, 1640, signed a marriage contract at Trois-Rivières to wed Marie Sédilot.[9] Bertrand's half brother François arrived in New France some twelve years after him and was a married man with children by the time he was counted in the first census taken in Canada in 1666. François is the direct ancestor of Joe Fafard.

The large Saskatchewan branch of the family was founded in the early twentieth century by the children of Dieudonné Fafard, three brothers and a sister, who were from the village of Saint-Germain-de-Grantham, near Drummondville, to the south of the Saint Lawrence River. The family farm was a long narrow strip of land that had to be drained to make it arable. The men farmed in the summer and worked in the lumber camps in the winter. Not large to begin with, the acreage was divided among the sons, leaving smaller and smaller parcels for successive genera-

7. Fafard has not lived in Pense since 1984, the year before he established a bronze foundry there and named it Julienne Atelier after his mother. He visits Pense daily to look after business and still participates in the life of the town

8. See *A Souvenir Album of Joe Fafard's Pensées*, the catalogue of a travelling exhibition, which originated at the Winnipeg Art Gallery in 1973 and was curated by Philip Fry and Bruce Ferguson.

9. See R. Jetté, *Dictionnaire généalogique des familles québécoises jusqu'en 1730* (Montreal: Presses de l'Université de Montréal, 1983), p. 409. A manuscript genealogy compiled by a member of the Fafard family notes that Bertrand was about twenty and Marie twelve when the contract was signed, and speculates that they did not marry until two or three years later. Their first child was born in 1645. Information on later family history has been provided by Joe Fafard.

tions. Around 1904, Alphonse, Fafard's paternal grandfather, and his two brothers struck out for Saskatchewan, where there was plentiful land for homesteading.

The three brothers settled near Crooked Lake at Grayson, a German-speaking community, and built a lodge to make ready for their families. Six years later, Alphonse Fafard and his wife Éliza (née Rajotte) moved to Sainte-Marthe, not far from Saint-Lazare, Manitoba, to form a community with other French-speaking settlers who were moving into Saskatchewan from Quebec. The Fafards and the Cantins were among the founding families of the village. When his parents moved to Sainte-Marthe, Léo Fafard, who was baptized Léopold, was just six months old. He grew up on the farm, and added to and farmed his father's land.[10] When Joe was eight years old, Léo bought the general store, which also contained the post office. Sainte-Marthe was located at the meeting point of four quarter-sections of Fafard land; owning the store put the family at the social centre of the community as well.

Fafard's maternal grandfather Joseph Cantin grew up in Saint-Raymond de Portneuf, west of Quebec City. Cantin worked in the lumber camps and tried his hand in the textile mills of New England before heading for Saskatchewan, around the same time as the Fafard brothers. Cantin married Colombe de Corby, a Saskatchewan woman who was born between two haystacks in the fields, to parents who came to the area directly from the south of France. Her father, Joseph de Corby, was a vine grower from the Ardèche. It fascinates Fafard that as a soldier in the Franco-Prussian War, his great-grandfather de Corby might have fought alongside the artists Manet and Degas during the Siege of Paris in 1870. It was not war, however, but an attack of phylloxera on his vineyards that convinced de Corby to leave France with his Basque wife (née Alvárez). They arrived in Saskatchewan in 1883 and settled in the wide, green Qu'Appelle Valley, a few kilometres north of Sainte-Marthe, which was up on the prairie, at a place found for them by Joseph's brother Jules de Corby. An Oblate father, Jules de Corby journeyed from France to Canada as a missionary in 1868 and became a colleague of Father Lacombe, the Church's spokesman for the Prairies. Father de Corby's correspondence, preserved by the Saskatchewan Archives Board, contains a mention of the birth of Fafard's grandmother, Colombe de Corby.

Joe Fafard was named for her husband Joseph Cantin, an adventurous, inventive man who enjoyed writing his own satirical verses to well-known tunes, such as the song he wrote about Sainte-Marthe to the melody of "The Yellow Rose of Texas", or another that poked fun at one of his daughter's suitors whom he disliked. (A penchant for satire and caricature is among his grandson's traits.) On both sides of Fafard's family, the culture is French for generations, intermingling the offshoots of old and New France with strains of French culture transformed by the Canadian West. Growing up in the Qu'Appelle Valley, Colombe de Corby, whose parents were educated, absorbed the rural Métis's distinctive culture by osmosis, observes Fafard, who is the only nonnative visual artist in the country to portray Métis people as members of the larger Canadian community. His Cantin and Fafard grandmothers, for all their lives, spoke only French. Two generations later, it was also the artist's mother tongue.

I started learning English when I started school in Sainte-Marthe, beginning with grade one. It was not a problem because everybody in the school spoke French. That first year, the teacher didn't speak French, but the older brothers and sisters would tell

10. The farm remains in the present generation of the family. Joe Fafard's parents recognized him as the artistic one from childhood, and when, at the age of twenty, he chose to enter university to study art, they gave him their blessing and their support.

you what the teacher said. She would just say, "Well, work in your books," and the older brothers and sisters would say, "This is the page you have to do." It just sort of was absorbed, like you get wet. I was nine years old the first time I consciously remember speaking English. A neighbour had come over who was English-speaking. By then we were running the store and he came to shop. He had brought his son along, who was my age, and they sent us out to play in the yard together. We treated people who came to the store to shop like they were guests. So we went out into the yard and sat on the steps of the granary and started talking. He would ask me questions and I remember I would answer as best I could. So he said to me, "When's your birthday?" and I said, "It's the two of September," and he laughed, "You don't say the two, you say the second." We learned a lot of English by reading Roy Rogers and Gene Autry comic books; we read those not because we were forced to but because we just wanted to. When we played cowboys, we would play in English, which we had practised: "Put up your hands!" and things like that. Then we'd switch back into French if we got into a discussion, like "Yes, yes, I shot you. You're dead!" We'd return to French because it was easier to play.

In *Wolf Willow*, Wallace Stegner describes his childhood world as "immediate, not comparative; seen flat, without perspective. Knowledge of place, knowledge of the past meant knowledge of the far and foreign."[11] Stegner grew up in a region deemed to be without history by the settlers who became its inhabitants. Fafard's childhood world, saturated with local knowledge, was almost exactly the opposite. Knowledge of place and the past meant knowledge of the family, which had been in Saskatchewan for three generations and in Quebec for nine. It also meant knowledge of Quebec, far enough away for the unseen relatives to seem like fictional characters, but not foreign. On the contrary, the Fafard clan felt like immigrants in their own country because of the distance from the mother culture, if not the mother country, from which this branch of the family, in effect, had emigrated.

So for comparison, on the far horizon, there was Quebec, and in Saskatchewan, there was the French-speaking community's cultural difference from its predominantly English-speaking neighbours. This was a built-in gauge from the moment Fafard started school. Having to negotiate his world in two languages gave it a perspective and dimension different from that of the family history. It pointed to parallel universes in which there were meeting places, and, perhaps, it strengthened his sense that there is a private interior world and a public exterior one.

The stories told in the intimacy of the family had their fictional counterparts on Radio-Canada in the 1940s and early 1950s. Broadcast on weekdays from Montreal, the immensely popular serialization of Quebec novelist Claude-Henri Grignon's *Un homme et son péché*, dramatized under the title *Les belles histoires des pays d'en haut*, was heard by French-speaking people across the country.[12] The fifteen-minute radio plays re-created the life of a northern Quebec village through its inhabitants and centred around the character Séraphin Poudrier, a miserly old habitant.

The fictional villagers and farmers seemed as vivid as the next-door neighbours, Fafard recalls, and when people gathered, they discussed the characters' antics and twists in the plot with the same conversational interest bestowed today on politics and sports. A citizen of Sainte-Marthe who exhibited the traits of one of Grignon's fictional characters could be sure to acquire his or her name by way of good-natured ribbing – someone who had a tight-fisted way with a dollar became a

11. Stegner 1977, p. 28.

12. *Les belles histoires des pays d'en haut* was broadcast on CBC Montreal from 1939 to 1962 and on CKVL Montreal from 1963 to 1965. In 1966, it was dramatized for television and ran as a TV show until 1970.

"Séraphin". Characterization was a constant of the social process in the culture of the Fafard family. Nicknames based on an individual's traits could even be found in the barnyard. Those who milked and herded cows, and harnessed and rode horses did not fail to observe these animals' personalities and temperaments. A family member could as easily be teased with the name of a recalcitrant cow as that of a character in the radio drama.

Incalculably pleasurable and mesmerizing because the voices seemed magically to be coming from nowhere, the radio fiction also was spoken in the familiar language of the village. Fafard first heard educated French spoken on the news broadcasts, which was evidence of yet another kind of outside world. The idea that there are worlds within worlds – the self within the world of family, the world of the family within the culture, French culture within Canada, animal world within human world (and vice versa), the past within the present-becoming-future, the fictional or fantastical within the world of oft-told "true" stories, and the mythological within the everyday – is germane to the imaginatively rich environment of Fafard's childhood and crucial to his art. Stories fed his active child's imagination. Still and all, as Gaston Bachelard, a philosopher of the creative imagination observes, the grown-up's stories are not the child's. "The child's imagination does not live from these fossil fables, these fossils of fables. The child finds his fables in his reverie, fables which he tells no one. Then the fable is life itself."[13] This capacity for reverie is the source of the poetic imagination: "In his solitudes, from the moment he is master of his reveries, the child knows the happiness of dreaming which will later be the happiness of poets."[14] The poetics of Fafard's visual art can also be said to spring from this capacity. In his own childhood daydreams and reveries, enhanced by a chance experience, Fafard imagined a miniature world within his everyday world which he looked down upon from the perspective of a sight-seer flying above an idyllic countryside.

When I was around the age of six, my father had an opportunity to send me up in a plane, at one of these small picnics where a guy, for so many dollars, would take up two people at a time. The Sainte-Marthe picnic was a baseball tournament. They would set up stands under the trees and serve ice cream and fruit and candies, and the neighbouring communities would play teams against each other. My father turned part of a field into a baseball diamond. He let the airplane land on his crop all that day. He sent me and a friend of mine who was five years old up in this plane. A lot of people went up, you know, and he was landing right in the field. So I went up and had a tour of Sainte-Marthe up in the air. You can imagine what that did to my six-year-old's imagination, to see all the familiar things from a totally different point of view. Because it's not like I was flying far or high. We flew all over things that I already knew and I recognized each cow in our milk herd, and from up there, it was suddenly no bigger than the little red cows that I played with. That, I found, was an amazing experience that stayed with me. I was still the same size, but the world had been reduced around me, as if suddenly you were Gulliver-among-the-Lilliputians in sensation.

I used to play a game in my mind when I was going to school, sitting and freezing in this van over a little sleigh. We travelled a mile and a half to school and, in those days, clothes were not as good as they are today in terms of keeping us warm, and this was an unheated thing. One of the games I played was to imagine a little horse and a little van

13. Gaston Bachelard, *The Poetics of Reverie: Childhood, Language and the Cosmos*, trans. Daniel Russell (Boston: Beacon Press, 1971), p. 118.

14. *Ibid.*, p. 99.

and sleigh very similar to the one I was in, but much smaller, say the horse would be about six or eight inches high. And in the ditch on the road, I would pick out a path that this little horse and sleigh would ride along and the obstacles it would have to overcome, and train my mind to see this phenomenon. I can still see it in the cold frozen snow, but the sun was shining on me. I was trying to keep myself warm and entertained and it was a real pleasure. Maybe that relates to this earlier experience of seeing the world from this flight in the air. I don't remember feeling scared. We had quite a bit of confidence that our father wasn't sending us to our deaths, but we were very moved by the whole thing.

Ma naissance, which embodies this miniaturizing, outside-looking-in point of view, suggests that even as an adult, for Fafard, it is French – the language in which he came to an awareness of the world, felt his emotional and perceptual life quicken, and immersed himself within his childhood reveries – that remains the language of his imagination, just as the Sainte-Marthe of his childhood remains its locus. What "art" did he know then? The calendar reproductions at home, the statues and holy pictures at church, the Christmas crèche with its miniature tableau of human and animal figures, the small carvings of horses made by a local man. The significant influences on Fafard's early work have been taken to be American: David Gilhooly, Robert Arneson and the California Funk ceramic movement. Beside them, one might also place all of the above and the seated figures of habitants by the wood-carver Médard Bourgault (1897-1967) of Saint-Jean-Port-Joli, the secular sculptures of Louis Jobin (1845-1928), to whom Fafard is related through his great-grandmother Victoria Jobin, and even the polychrome ceramic wall plaques by Édouard Jasmin (1905-1987), which typically picture comical vignettes of

Fig. 5. *Asleep in His Mother's House*, 1988 (cat. 28)

fantastical and everyday events.[15] Believing that language is a container and transmitter of culture, Fafard acknowledges a connection to Quebec artists like these, even though their work was not known to him at the beginning of his career in the 1970s.

I think it might be contained in language, somehow, quite mysteriously. It's hard to say, but it's not like it always has to have a visual precedent to show up, because one of the things I have for sure in common with these people is the language. It was the rural life, the habitant's way of speaking. I think that also colours the way you see the world; you know, how you think and perceive, and relate to other people in terms of what you say to them. It might be that the visual phenomenon is dependent on language as well. And I don't mean by that the sounds of language but the expressions and the idioms of the language. The language is full of images. There are all kinds of images in the language that would have been shared right across French Canada.

Asleep in His Mother's House (fig. 5), a work from the middle of Fafard's career, reaffirms his deep feeling of connection to the mother culture and mother tongue. Made the year after Julienne Fafard's death, the small bronze sculpture can be read as a reverie on the mother, a reverie towards childhood, embodied by the figure of an adult dreamer asleep on a couch. The phrase "reverie towards childhood" belongs to Bachelard, who uses it when speaking of the adult poet, deep in the solitude of reverie which returns him to the original solitude of childhood. Here, a bearded man lies exhausted across the couch, his head resting on the upholstered arm in a horizontal figure composition with only one echo in Fafard's oeuvre: the emerging newborn of *Ma naissance*. Red-nosed and slack-jawed, the grown man is sound asleep, his body heavy with the gravitational pull of an adult's world. Yet the dark blue-green leaf-patterned couch trimmed with wood holds him as though it were a forest nest or a womb.

"The very nature of the dreamer's language has shaped the reverie," the translator of *The Poetics of Reverie*, Daniel Russell, writes.[16] And here, the couch may hint at a pun: the word "couch" lies embedded in "accouchement", the French for "childbirth". Thus, the adult dreamer of *Asleep in His Mother's House* contains the idea of *Ma naissance*, the dreaming infant coming into the world which Fafard singled out as the point of origin for his work. The artist's reverie embodied by *Asleep in His Mother's House* is a reverie towards childhood and, at the same time, a reverie towards the source, the origins of his life and work.

Fafard himself relates the dreaming figure in *Asleep in His Mother's House* to Vincent van Gogh, the legendary Dutch artist,[17] with whom he has identified and whom he has represented in a series of sculptures dating from 1982 to 1987, the longest series he has made on a single subject other than the cow. In this work, Fafard pictures Van Gogh dreaming in a sleep of renewal. But this work is unlike any of Fafard's other Van Goghs, all of which re-imagine the artist through his painting and inhabit a clearly fictional realm. The narrative time of *Asleep in His Mother's House* is more ambiguous. The dark hair and beard, the shirt and trousers which could be contemporary, and the forties-style couch invite a parallel reading of the sleeping man as a self-portrait of the dark-haired, bearded Fafard. Perhaps, *Asleep in His Mother's House* portrays the artist, emptied by grief, seeking sanctuary in order to restore himself. For in the words of Bachelard, "In our reverie which imagines while remembering our past takes on substance again."[18]

15. See Pascale Galipeau, *Les Paradis du monde : l'art populaire au Québec* (Hull: Musée canadien des civilisations, 1995).

16. Bachelard 1971, p. vi.

17. So legendary a figure is Van Gogh that a French sociologist has recently written a study of the construction of the image of Van Gogh and its ramifications for the image of the modern artist. See Nathalie Heinich, *The Glory of Van Gogh: An Anthropology of Admiration* (Princeton, New Jersey: Princeton University Press, 1996).

18. Bachelard 1971, p. 119. *Asleep in His Mother's House* served as the maquette for the self-portrait *The Inventor on His Invention* (cat. 29).

The difference between these images of reverie from the artist's youth and his middle age is this: *Ma naissance*, with the gigantic baby that by definition is grotesque, suggests the reverie towards childhood by what it embodies, while *Asleep in His Mother's House*, with its normative image of restorative sleep, does so not just by what it embodies but also through what cannot be pictured, alluding to it in the curled position of the dreamer's body and in the protective, maternal, interior space summoned up by the title. "That which most properly belongs to the sanctuary of childhood, and the childlike, proves grotesque when conflated with the actuality of the phenomenal world," writes Lynne Cooke. "If by its very nature a sanctuary is dependent on what it excludes for its sense of self, the reality it encloses cannot be easily equated with what it keeps out. The fragility of the distinctions that demarcate the terrain of childhood from the adult world is revealed over and over, and with it a sense of the precariousness and dubiousness of the values that divorce one from the other."[19] If on the outside, *Asleep in His Mother's House* appears to accentuate the cares of the adult world, the location of the dreamer within this sanctuary also reaffirms the poetic terrain of childhood that continues to nourish Fafard's work. Its signs are to be found everywhere in the dialectic between the small and the large, the interior and the exterior, the near and the far, the intimate and the public, the realms of everyday life and exaggeration, and wonder and jest.

The roots of Fafard's imagination have taken hold in literary soil common to the vernacular and to high art. Each of his figures, human or animal, denotes a character whose presence and physical description imply a story with a narrative connection to other characters and thus to a world larger than itself alone. If the Fafard family's oral culture offers one model and Grignon's radio dramatization suggests another, a third exemplar set on the Prairies is the Canadian novelist Margaret Laurence's creation of Manawaka, the fictional place inhabited by Scottish settlers and Métis, which Laurence based on her hometown, Neepawa, Manitoba.[20] Fafard, however, is a visual artist, a sculptor who must give bodies to characters and render them without a linear plot. The sign of his poetic reveries can be read, especially, in his uses of two devices most often thought of as belonging to different disciplines, the writer's point of view and the visual artist's sense of scale, which in Fafard's work are linked intimately in the construction of a microcosm.

When I started doing those pieces [with the bird's-eye perspectives], in particular, I didn't go up in the air, but it was a point of view that one could assume and imagine from. You don't try to make things realistic, you just re-create from that point of view. Perhaps it's the same way that a writer, when they write from within a character, for instance, has to assume that point of view and write from there. Eventually, they say the character has a voice and all they have to do is listen to the character speak with his voice and that they don't actually invent anything. Therefore if they can get in character, the thoughts come to them that a character would have. So those things are like assuming a point of view which is a hundred feet up in the air, and being able to see the whole from there, and then working away at the surface from that point of view like you're not in that point of view.[21]

The viewpoint from a hundred feet in the air presents the world in miniature. Fafard works in a wide range of sizes, from two inches to twenty feet, with allusions that invoke both miniature and gigantic scale, extremes that Bachelard recognizes

19. Lynne Cooke, "Micromegas", *Parkett*, vol. 44 (1995), p. 135.

20. Fafard modelled a clay portrait figure of Laurence in 1980, one of several he has made of Canadian writers. See *Joe Fafard (and...)*, (Toronto: Gallery Moos, 1981), an exhibition brochure with short essays by Saskatchewan poets Patrick Lane and Lorna Uher, who is now known as Lorna Crozier.

21. The works in which Fafard depicts an explicit bird's-eye perspective are found among his prints, such as the screenprints *Bird* (1977) and *DC Neuf* (1978). The humorous *Bird* shows a sunny overhead "bird's-eye view" of nine cows standing in a paddock rendered as a boxlike geometric illusion. In the nighttime view of *DC Neuf*, the Earth, shaped like an egg, is seen suspended in black space and illuminated only by the traceries of light from expressways and cloverleaf exchanges. "Neuf" is French for both "new" and "nine", and the title, in referring to the DC-9 aircraft, perhaps alludes through language to Fafard's memory of his first plane ride over Sainte-Marthe. The image combines the child's and the adult's points of view in the depiction of a no longer arcadian industrialized landscape, which nonetheless appears wondrous from this distant perspective.

as compatible and capable of existing one inside the other.[22] Yet, it is in miniaturization that Fafard's initial conception of a microcosm lies, a world within a world that is both a double mirror (of the world and of the mind perceiving the world) and an aesthetic invention. One might even say that the miniature horse and sleigh paralleling and warming Fafard's freezing rides to school was an aesthetic invention or its seed. In her book *On Longing: Narratives of the Miniature, the Gigantic, the Souvenir, the Collection*, Susan Stewart observes, "There are no miniatures in nature; the miniature is a cultural product, the product of an eye performing certain operations, manipulating, and attending in certain ways to, the physical world."[23] The miniature also exhibits several manifestations as a cultural form, physically and in literature. The literary cousins of Fafard's vision might include the tale of Le Petit Poucet, or Tom Thumb, or, inversely, the tall tales of Paul Bunyan. In the physical world, however, the miniature form most relevant to the origins of Fafard's work is the toy.

Looking down from the airplane, Fafard gained a transforming perspective and perceived a worldful of living beings on the scale of his toys. "The toy is the physical embodiment of the fiction: it is a device for fantasy, a point of beginning for narrative," Stewart writes. "The toy opens an interior world, lending itself to fantasy and privacy in a way that the abstract space, the playground, of social play does not. To toy with something is to manipulate it, to try it out within sets of contexts, none of which is determinative."[24] One might say that the child's play is a rehearsal for the creative play of the mature artist. "The inanimate toy repeats the still life's theme of arrested life, the life of the tableau. But once the toy becomes animated [in this case, by the imagination] it initiates another world, the world of the daydream."[25]

This is the world of reverie, and what is the atmosphere of this daydream but a longing which the artist can attempt to fulfil and transcend? "That the world of things can open itself to reveal a secret life – indeed, to reveal a set of actions and hence a narrativity and history outside the given field of perception . . . This is the daydream of the microscope: the daydream of life inside life, of significance multiplied infinitely *within* significance."[26] By no means a realist sculptor, Fafard intensifies the uncanny quality of his three-dimensional figures by giving them an otherworldly miniaturized scale. They might seem ready – as in the children's game called statues – to complete arrested gestures as soon as one's back is turned. They might even seem on the verge of speech. But they mean to fool no one. They seek to enchant and to challenge the eye and body of the beholder. Stewart writes that "The toy world presents a projection of everyday life; this real world is miniaturized or giganticized in such a way as to test the relation between materiality and meaning."[27] In a sense, this is what all representational sculpture does, but it is particularly true of the cast of characters that populates Fafard's fiction, which seems to slow down time, to disrupt linear timelines and to possess the ability to entertain shifting points of view.

Implicit within the miniature and the gigantic, point of view is the crux of Fafard's work. How one sees the world depends upon a point of view formed in relation to language, culture, images and experience. Fafard, like Stegner, mixes autobiography with history and fiction to give the fullest account. He expresses his cultural difference in his point of view and acknowledges that everyone sees the world in a different way. He is interested in these differences. They contain stories. In his dual role of author and observer, he becomes both master and servant of all

22. Gaston Bachelard, *The Poetics of Space*, trans. Maria Jolas (Boston: Beacon Press, 1969), p. 172.

23. Susan Stewart, *On Longing: Narratives of the Miniature, the Gigantic, the Souvenir, the Collection* (Durham and London: Duke University Press, 1993), p. 55.

24. *Ibid.*, p. 56.

25. *Ibid.*, p. 57.

26. *Ibid.*, p. 54.

27. *Ibid.*, p. 57.

he surveys. Yet, his sights are set on another realm that lies, like the horizon, always at a distance. This is a paradox of Fafard's sculpture: it inhabits real space, but it is "out of time". The urge to embody what he portrays by actually giving it *a body* contains the ancient desire to memorialize and mirror life through art, to seek transcendence of temporality in the timeless. The miniature removes the viewer absorbed by its detail and its visual all-at-onceness into "the infinite time of reverie".[28]

"In a world where access to speed is access to transcendence," Stewart writes, "point of view is particularly a narrative gesture."[29] It has made a storyteller of Joe Fafard.

28. *Ibid.*, pp. 65-69. Stewart cites an experiment that suggests "there may be an actual phenomenological correspondence between the experience of scale and the experience of duration". This transformed sense of time marks the invention of what Stewart calls "private time": "In other words, miniature time transcends the duration of everyday life in such a way as to create an interior temporality of the subject" (see page 66).

29. *Ibid.*, p. 3.

The Pasture

Fig. 1. *The Pasture*, 1984-1985 (cat. 34)

Joe Fafard's largest outdoor sculpture, *The Pasture* (fig. 1), invokes the agricultural landscape in the heart of the city simply by placing seven larger-than-life-size bronze cows on a patch of grass amid the office buildings of Toronto's financial district. The whole work consists entirely of the cows. Each is a free-standing sculpture, so to speak, that sits without a base directly on the ground, with front legs folded back and bulky haunches rolled to one side. The setting completes the piece, whose "nature" would change if it were placed in any other context. In every sense, *The Pasture* is a site-specific work. It operates by intervening in the cityscape. It brings the country into the city at no less pointed a location than Toronto-Dominion Centre, a huge plaza boasting a cluster of austere black Mies van der Rohe office towers. It juxtaposes *cows* with a paragon of architectural modernism, placing these signs of regionalism cheek by jowl with the most comprehensive monument of the International Style in Canada, built by one of the country's largest banking corporations.

The imagery and context of *The Pasture* summon up the sometimes provocative relationship between the East and West of Canada, the farmer and the banker, the family farm and the stock exchange, as well as the interdependence of the city and the country in relation to the food supply. The associations are historical, financial, political, social and ecological. They speak to origins[1] and to the prudent management of resources for the future. The number of cows, seven, is a cautionary biblical reference. In Genesis, when Joseph interprets the Pharaoh's dream of watching seven lean cows swallow seven fat ones and seven thin ears of corn devour seven full

1. See Peter White, "Mythic Marvels", in *Joe Fafard: Cows and Other Luminaries, 1977-1987* (Saskatoon: Mendel Art Gallery, 1987), p. 20. "At the heart of the regionalist impulse is the question of origins," writes White. "In *The Pasture*, Fafard transposed his [origins] to invest that urban, commercial site with its own rural beginnings."

ears as the portent of famine, he is appointed administrator of food and stores in preparation for the time of want. And there is more to find in the juxtaposition. What greater contrast in form can be imagined than that of sleek modernist buildings' hard skins of glass, metal and granite with the organic combination of bony angles, bunched muscles and soft-tissue bulges that constitutes bovine anatomy? The latter seems to beg the question of which form really follows function, almost to rebuke modernist values for being so far removed from the actuality of life. What could be more antithetical to the serene unconcerned animality of these creatures on the grassy field than the hustle and bustle of the city streets?

It is as though the consciousness of one leviathan, the vast Prairie, has invaded another, the sprawling Modern Metropolis, through these humble emissaries. The body of the cow is the part that stands for the whole, the prairie landscape. Monumentalized by larger-than-life-size scale and by bronze, a material associated with heroic sculpture, the cows are not themselves gigantic; they invoke the gigantic body of the land, and the colossal but relative scale of their urban setting is put into perspective by their presence. "We find the miniature at the origin of private, individual history, but we find the gigantic at the origin of public and natural history," Susan Stewart writes. "The gigantic becomes an explanation for the environment, a figure on the interface between the natural and the human."[2] Moreover, Fafard embeds the private in the public, the close-up and the far point of view, in this commission for Toronto-Dominion Centre, placing on the interface of his own interactions with nature the figure of the animal. Each cast from the same mould, the seven cows depict a small herd at rest – a phenomenon that Fafard based on "many childhood experiences" of taking "a leisurely walk in the pasture".[3]

"There I observed nature undisturbed," he writes in "The Pasture: A Proposal to Bring Cows to Downtown Toronto". "A small herd of milk cows, quiet and woven into the landscape, was always the focal point. They became the connection between humans and the land. They were part of nature, yet they were ours. We exploited them, yet assured their survival and well being. We spent much of our summer working to assure their food supply for the coming winter. In winter we housed, fed and cleaned them. In return we drew much of our food directly from their bodies. A symbiotic relationship between us and them has been established for thousands of years. It continues today and will continue tomorrow. The city dweller is no less involved, just less directly involved."[4]

Nature undisturbed: a far cry from the pristine, sublime, alien or threatening wilderness perceived by the explorers and earliest settlers, Fafard's view of nature is akin to that of the farmer who looks out over an agricultural landscape inhabited by people who have animals and crops to sustain them. Embodied by his figures of animals – cows, calves, bulls, horses and colts – Fafard's conception of the landscape contains the notions of work, productivity, ownership and good husbandry. This is "the working landscape" that Rosemary Donegan identifies in *Work, Weather and the Grid: Agriculture in Saskatchewan* as a "distinctive imagery of prairie agriculture",[5] a form of the pastoral derived from fine art and folk art, which has developed since the settlement period at the turn of the century.

The pastoral has ancient literary roots in the *Idyls* of Theocritus and Vergil's *Georgics*, a didactic poem in four books about agriculture. In the visual and decorative arts, the georgic tradition celebrated farming and rural work. "As a highly developed pastoral genre, it could be seen in paintings, graphics, illustrations, and

2. Susan Stewart, *On Longing: Narratives of the Miniature, the Gigantic, the Souvenir, the Collection* (Durham and London: Duke University Press, 1993), p. 71.

3. Joe Fafard, "The Pasture: A Proposal to Bring Cows to Downtown Toronto," *Brick*, no. 25 (Fall 1985), p. 28.

4. *Ibid.*

5. Rosemary Donegan, *Work, Weather and the Grid: Agriculture in Saskatchewan* (Regina: Dunlop Art Gallery, 1991), pp. 6, 8.

ceramics and was exemplified in the work of the English artist John Constable (1776-1837) and earlier in the Italianate landscape painting of Claude Lorrain (1600-1682),"[6] Donegan writes. Among its subjects were "the magnificence of the estate and the splendor of animals upon it". Georgic imagery "served to validate the importance of farming for the general wealth of society". Among its Saskatchewan practitioners, Donegan places self-taught artists like Jan Wyers and W. C. McCargar, as well as Fafard, Victor Cicansky, Russell Yuristy and David Thauberger – younger trained artists who came to prominence in the 1970s and were influenced by Funk Art and Pop Art (and, one must add, by the work of senior self-taught artists like Wyers and McCargar) to bring new approaches to the working landscape.

An equally if not more important aspect of the idea of the pastoral for Fafard, and for Cicansky and Thauberger, all of whom have chosen to base their work on everyday personal and regional experience, is this: "Traditionally, the name given to [the] incorporation of the commonplace within the exalted – and vice-versa – has been pastoral,"[7] writes Thomas Crow, who cites William Empson's literary criticism of the 1930s as the basis for the modern idea of the pastoral. Empson, he says, identified "the persistent form of modern pastoral, which replaces the chivalrous shepherd of earlier times, as the ironic joining of 'the idea of everything being included in the ruling hero' to 'the idea of everything being included in the humble thing, with mystical respect for poor men, fools and children.'"[8] The rediscovery of European pastoralism in modern art, Crow writes, "allowed a distinctive voice to be constructed from the pastoral contrast between large artistic ambitions and a simultaneous awareness – figured through the surrogate of the child and consciously childish activities – of everyone's limited horizons and modest powers. Through this ironic reduction of the heroic point of view (the child is powerless but gives the power once again to observe the world), they managed to recover figuration."[9]

The Pasture is a brilliant contemporary embodiment of pastoral contrast, of which "The most traditional is between the little world of natural simplicity and the great world of civilization, power, statecraft, ordered society, established codes of behavior, and artifice in general."[10] Nowhere is the conceptual field of Fafard's work so clearly to be seen as here. The replication of a single cow represents the herd, and the herd invokes the landscape, which is a landscape of a particular kind. Indeed, a single Fafard cow does this on its own. It carries the pastoral with it wherever it goes.

The cow was the first creature that Fafard modelled in clay, and it has been the constant in his work. Apparently simple and straightforward, it is a vehicle for complexities. Not only is it the figure with which Fafard invokes the prairie landscape; the cow marks a point at which metaphysics and utility come together in his work. "Why Look at Animals?" John Berger asks in an essay: "What were the secrets of the animal's likeness with, and unlikeness from man? The secrets whose existence man recognized as soon as he intercepted an animal's look?"[11] He answers, "All the secrets were about animals as an *intercession* between man and his origins . . . Animals came from over the horizon. They belonged *there* and *here*. Likewise they were mortal and immortal. An animal's blood flowed like human blood, but its species was undying and each lion was Lion, each ox was Ox. This – maybe the first existential dualism – was reflected in the treatment of animals. They were subjected *and* worshipped, bred *and* sacrificed."[12] Modern society everywhere but in rural

6. *Ibid.*, p. 8.

7. Thomas Crow, *Modern Art in the Common Culture* (New Haven and London: Yale University Press, 1996), p. 176.

8. *Ibid.*, p. 180. Empson is quoted from *Some Versions of the Pastoral*, revised edition (New York: New Editions, 1974).

9. Crow 1996, p. 182. Crow refers specifically to Rauschenberg and Johns (and includes Duchamp), who eschewed the heroic rhetoric of the Abstract Expressionists, bringing concrete evidence of everyday life into their work through the use of the found object and the readymade and influencing a generation of Pop artists. Theoretically, however, his observations on the workings of the modern pastoral can also be applied to Fafard, Cicansky, Yuristy and Thauberger, who two decades later were developing distinctive voices steeped in popular culture in opposition to the abstract New York-influenced colour-field painting, which held sway in Saskatchewan in the 1970s.

10. David Halperin, *Before Pastoral: Theocritus and the Ancient Tradition of Bucolic Poetry* (New Haven and London: Yale University Press, 1983), pp. 70-77, quoted from Crow 1996, p. 256, note 12.

11. John Berger, "Why Look at Animals?", in *About Looking* (New York: Pantheon Books, 1980), p. 4.

12. *Ibid.*, pp. 4-5.

Fig. 2. *Smoothly She Shifted*, 1986/1987 (cat. 39)

peasant cultures has marginalized animals into invisibility, Berger concludes, and without them human beings are alone. "Today the vestiges of this dualism remain among those who live intimately with, and depend upon, animals."[13] Perhaps this is why, in the fictional pastoral world of Fafard's making, the intimacy between human beings and animals is so steadfastly maintained.

At the same time, the cow is the only form that Fafard manipulates constantly, using the oldest subject of art, the animal, as the basis for restless formal experimentation. It is as though the inclusiveness of the modern pastoral opens the door to both popular and high art excursions in Fafard's art, which rests in all of its manifestations on the strata of art history. The cows of *The Pasture* call to mind everything from Pompeiian frescoes to the illuminations in medieval books of hours to Renaissance nativity scenes and seventeenth-century Dutch landscapes. When arranged in a staggered overlapping line, the five *Assyrian Cows* (1987) (cat. 40) invoke Egyptian relief sculptures as well as nineteenth-century tradesmen's signs and lead toys. Cows that warp in space like the folded accordion of *Foreshortened Standing Cow* (1985/1986) (cat. 35), which appears fully three-dimensional from the front, and *Smoothly She Shifted* (fig. 2) demonstrate the ways point of view affects perception.

Fig. 3. *Altamira I*, 1991 (cat. 53)

Altamira I (fig. 3) and *Vie en Vie I* (1991) (cat. 56) are bronze outlines, drawings in air that incorporate their surroundings. And *Gris*, which bends the bronze outlines of a bull into three dimensions and is named for a Spanish Cubist painter, folds up succinctly as one moves around it into an all but completely abstract view of just eight lines (see p. 9). With its stages of transformation from representation to abstraction, *Gris* recalls not only Picasso's *Le taureau* (1945-1946), a lithograph in eleven states that progressively reduce the image, but also Roy Lichtenstein's "Bull" series (1973), lithographs inspired by *Le taureau* in which an illustrator's bull becomes a sophisticated tongue-in-cheek Pop-Cubist's abstract design.

13. See Jean Lipman and Richard Marshall, *Art about Art*, with an introduction by Leo Steinberg (New York: E.P. Dutton, 1978), pp. 118-119.

Leo Steinberg once referred to this kind of activity as "rustling". Among Fafard's often playful and parodistic experiments there are bulls whose mien suggests the mythic, horses whose sturdy forms bow to Uccello, Dürer and Lautrec, and cows whose attributes come partly from cards showing the characteristics of breeds and partly from invention. Between artists' "experience of nature and their experience of other art, they allow no functional difference," Steinberg writes. "Foraging where they live – that is to say among precedents – they exploit their environment and, like all living organisms, avail themselves."[14]

This rich and sustaining environment, which spreads out all around them like a pasture, is the history of art. It is the landscape of culture, nature's complement, in which Fafard also takes many a "leisurely walk". Going still further afield, Fafard has enlisted nature to imprint culture directly onto the land in a work-in-progress commissioned for the International Plowing Match in Simcoe County, Ontario, in the summer of 1997. In this work, six hundred metres long and more than three hundred wide, the figure of an enormous draft horse will be planted in winter wheat, harvested to a golden stubble and surrounded by a landscape painted in the hues of peas and corn and canola. So gigantic will this spectacle be that to view it, one must stand on a knoll, climb to the top of an adjacent tower, rise aloft in a tethered hot-air balloon or fly above it in a light plane, as Fafard once flew over a picnic in Sainte-Marthe.

14. *Ibid.*, p. 10.

Dear Vincent

The allusive title of *Dear Vincent* (fig.1, cats. 1-3) is an epistolary salutation and a term of endearment; the work itself, an intense homage to Vincent van Gogh. Fafard imagines him sitting in a cane-bottom chair, clutching a palette and brushes in one hand and, in the other, a lighted candle and a brush loaded with luminous yellow paint. Through the title, he evokes Van Gogh the writer and recipient of letters, whose voluminous correspondence with his brother Theo constitutes one of the most remarkable documents we have of an artist's life.[1] Perhaps the sculpture is Fafard's letter to Vincent, describing in the vividly immediate sensuous terms of sculptor's and painter's materials his feelings towards the painter who believed so strongly that colour is light and who yearned to found a utopian artists' colony in the south of France.

Depicting Vincent as a figure holding a lighted candle, Fafard gives him the iconography of Faith. He textures the entire surface of the sculpture – skin, hair, clothing, chair – with the impasto of painting, interweaving brush strokes of flickering complementary colours. The Vincent that Fafard portrays is the revolutionary Vincent of Arles, Saint-Rémy and Auvers showing the way to others through his art – visionary, as ethereal as a vision, and yet as corporeal and as solid as a rock. It is as though the Dutch artist's figure has materialized from the stuff of one of his own paintings to assume this three-dimensional presence. He seems not to be frozen and immutable as some sculptures do but to be knitting his brow in concentration and tensing for the next move. Robert Enright aptly noted that Fafard's figures can "seem to be contemplating their own existence in space".[2] How true this is of *Dear Vincent*, which appears to spring from pigment wielded in Van Gogh's style into an embodied figment of Fafard's imagination. How appropriate it is that this figure alludes to Van Gogh as both a painter and a writer.

Dear Vincent, the title, which already introduces words into the equation, suggests that the sculpture is a text. "Writing, in its physical, graphic form, is an inseparable suturing of the visual and the verbal, the 'imagetext' incarnate," W.J.T. Mitchell writes.[3] Beyond this supreme example, he proposes that "all arts are 'composite' arts (both text and image); all media are mixed media, combining different codes, discursive conventions, channels, sensory and cognitive modes."[4] Moreover, in the case of images, the texts appropriate for comparison are "already inside the image, perhaps more deeply when they seem to be most completely absent, invisible and inaudible".[5] All of Fafard's three-dimensional figures, then, informed by stories, fables, tall tales, biography, memoires and anecdotal histories, are images and texts combined.

Human or animal, the figures look outward as though contemplating or responding to the presence of a viewer, or appear to cast their gaze inward as though contemplating themselves. In either eventuality, Fafard so strongly evokes

Fig. 1. *Dear Vincent*, 1983 (cat. 1)

1. During the period when Fafard was making the Van Gogh sculptures, he read the artist's letters and every biography he could find. The popular edition of the letters is *Dear Theo*, selected by the novelist Irving Stone, which Fafard echoes in the title of *Dear Vincent*.

2. Robert Enright, "Working in the Flatland: An Interview with Joe Fafard", *Border Crossings*, vol. 7, no. 1 (January 1988), p. 11.

3. W.J.T. Mitchell, *Picture Theory: Essays on Verbal and Visual Representation* (Chicago and London: University of Chicago Press, 1994), p. 95.

4. *Ibid.*, pp. 94-95.

5. *Ibid.*, p. 98.

self-awareness or self-consciousness that the figurative object becomes transformed into a subject. This animated, uncanny presence, as much as iconography or description, gives Fafard's figures the sense that they are characters inhabiting a narrative. No unfolding of a plot is necessary to satisfy the minimum conditions for narrativity. "That what is implicitly or explicitly told must take time hardly distinguishes narrative," Nelson Goodman writes, "for even description or depiction of a momentary and static situation implies something of what went before and will come afterward."[6] The connotations of arrested or imminent movement in expression, gesture or pose – characterizations which Fafard heightens by making the head and the hands, the most expressive parts of the body, the largest – imply the future and the past.

Solidly within the viewer's space, the figures also seem to dwell simultaneously in "real" time and a parallel eternal present. Viewers construct their own narrative accounts in the phenomenological encounter with the sculpture of a single figure. The event is slowed by contemplation and made sequential by moving around the figure and seeing it in its parts and from shifting points of view. The narrative arrives in the lived time of the perceiver's imagination, as in Paul Hernadi's observation: "It seems to me that a narrative sequence requires the lived time of the perceiver's imagination if it is to evoke the narrated events with a temporal dimension of their own."[7] But in Fafard's sculptures of the art critic Clement Greenberg and the artists Van Gogh and Cézanne, a significant aspect of the event narrated by perception concerns the dialogue between painting and sculpture, as well as the visual counterpoint between the means of pictorial illusion and the means of perceptual illusion in one and the same object.

Fafard made the first of the Van Gogh sculptures, which number more than fifty when the forty painted clay plaques in the remarkable *Vincent Self-portrait Series* (cat. 8) are counted, in 1982, two years into his investigations of illusion combining the effects of sculpture and painting.[8] Ideas such as these were in the air. In the 1960s and 1970s, Picasso and Dubuffet made gigantic public sculptures that actualized images and surfaces from their paintings in three-dimensions. Artists have been a subject of art since Antiquity. Contemporary art, in particular, is filled with representations of old and modern masters and parodies of their styles. Images of Van Gogh and quotations from his paintings have appeared in the work of many artists, such as Canadians Murray Favro and Ron Moppett and Americans Red Grooms and Robert Arneson.

Contact with Arneson could easily be what led Fafard to return to the relief plaque, this time as wall-mounted portrait heads, similar to plaques the California artist was making in the seventies. The basic form, however, is a common one – the commercially manufactured plaster plaque made to decorate the walls of kitchens and living rooms. Both artists found the plaque attractive for its accessibility as a low-brow form. Despite the vast disparities in their styles and points of view, there is an affinity between Fafard's and Arneson's work. Arneson made portrait sculptures of his artist contemporaries, such as Roy De Forest, David Gilhooly, William T. Wiley and Peter Voulkos, and of his artist heroes Picasso, Marcel Duchamp, Francis Bacon and Jackson Pollock.[9] Fafard's portraits of artists begin with the older, self-taught W. C. McCargar, Regina friends like Russell Yuristy and Torontonian Michael Snow, and move on to Rousseau, Van Gogh, Cézanne, Monet, Renoir and Picasso. Fafard has even made a sculpture portraying Arneson making a

6. Nelson Goodman, "Twisted Tales; or, Story, Study, and Symphony," in W.J.T. Mitchell, ed., *On Narrative* (Chicago and London: University of Chicago Press, 1981), p. 111.

7. Paul Hernadi, "Afterthoughts on Narrative 1: On the How, What, and Why of Narrative," in Mitchell 1981, p. 197.

8. Fafard relates the beginnings of these experiments to reading E. H. Gombrich's *Art and Illusion* for the first time in 1980 in preparation for working with students as a visiting artist at the University of California at Davis. He was undoubtedly invigorated as well by time spent in the company of artists at this hub of the California clay movement, where Robert Arneson was teaching and David Gilhooly and Victor Cicansky had studied.

9. For this and other references to Arneson's work, see Neal Benezra, *Robert Arneson: A Retrospective* (Des Moines: Des Moines Art Center, 1986). Born in 1930, Arneson died of cancer in 1991.

self-portrait, *Arneson and Bob* (1980). Arneson's plaque of Bacon mimics the British artist's painting, but *Jackson Pollock* (1983), a portrait plaque painted with drips and splatters, comes closest to the Van Goghs that Fafard had begun the previous year. The difference is that the Pollock wears the drips on its surface like a veil over the face, while the Van Gogh plaques appear to be lifted right out of the paintings and drawings. *Dear Vincent* is a composite, the chair taken from one painting, the boots from another, and so on. Each face in the *Vincent Self-portrait Series* represents one of the forty self-portraits Van Gogh made in his lifetime, rendered, as it were, in his own "handwriting".

Fafard gives the figures of his artist friends the character-animating proportions of caricature, but avoids distorting the human form as radically as he does the malleable forms of cows or the sculptures of Van Gogh and Cézanne. In the Van Goghs especially, he takes the painting-as-sculpture/sculpture-as-painting analogies as far as he can push them, manifesting the space of painting, its perspective and foreshortenings, in sculptures like the clay *Vincent (Japanese)* (fig. 2), the bronze *The Painter* (1986) (cat. 11) and the big, hollowed-out bronze head *Vincent* (1982/1986) (cat. 6). The strangest and most haunting are the plaques of the *Vincent Self-portrait Series*. The disembodied face, often unsupported by neck and shoulders or even the frill of a shirt collar, makes an unusual subject for sculpture. The plaques emphasize the analogy between portrait and mask, and point to the fluidity of the self, a "character" that not even its owner sees in the same way twice. "If the surface is the location of the body's meaning, it is because that surface is invisible to the body itself," Susan Stewart writes. "And if the face reveals a depth and profundity which the body is not capable of, it is because the eyes and to some degree the mouth are openings onto fathomlessness . . . The face is a type of 'deep' text, a text whose meaning is complicated by change and by a constant series of alterations between a reader and an author who is strangely disembodied, neither present nor absent, found in neither part nor whole, but, in fact, *created* by this reading."[10] Re-creating his images and his brush strokes, Fafard searches for Van Gogh the author in order to transcend himself in his own place and time.

"I'm trying to find some kind of reflection on the life that we had, and I don't mean me, I mean people as a whole," Fafard once said. "So that when I'm doing a portrait, I feel a bit like a writer who is evoking a character, I feel a bit like an actor who is interpreting a character, I feel like an artist who's making a portrait."[11] In the studio, he assumes a figure's stance, feeling the set of the limbs and the distribution of weight through his own body. He begins the internalized conversation with the subject that draws the character out. In the process, there is an invocation. There is a deep sense that certain of Fafard's figures are effigies as much as portraits – his parents and grandparents, the Métis and Native figures that invoke the history of Saskatchewan, and the portraits of Van Gogh, Cézanne, Monet, Renoir and Picasso, which construe a brotherhood in the history of art. It has been said that Fafard is gathering his ancestral figures around him. After reading Van Gogh's letters and accounts of his life and work, Fafard said, "I felt a bit like a novice studying the lives of the saints."

The first time Fafard discovered there was such a thing as perceptual illusion in sculpture, he was an altar boy cleaning the dust off the saints in the Catholic church in Sainte-Marthe. These polychrome statues, descended from the Middle Ages and the Renaissance, were proportioned to appeal to the eye seeing them from below.

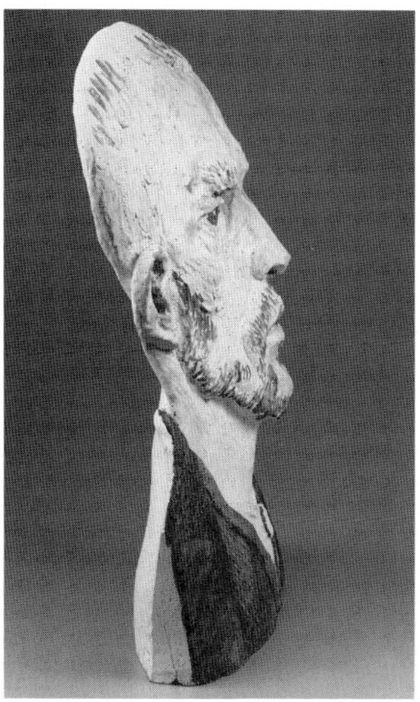

Fig. 2. Two views of *Vincent (Japanese)*, 1982 (cat. 9)

10. Susan Stewart, *On Longing: Narratives of the Miniature, the Gigantic, the Souvenir, the Collection* (Durham and London: Duke University Press, 1993), p. 127.

11. Enright 1988, p. 17.

As Umberto Eco writes of medieval exemplars, "The statues in the King's Gallery in Amiens Cathedral were designed to be seen from a floor thirty metres below; the eyes were placed far from the nose, and the hair sculpted in great masses. At Rheims, statues on the spires have arms that are too short, backs that are too long, lowered shoulders, and short legs. The demands of objective proportion were subordinated to the demands of the eye."[12] Again it is a matter of point of view. The demands of objective proportion in Fafard's figures are subordinated to the demands of his subjective response to their subjects, nowhere so much as in the sculptures of Van Gogh. Fafard compares his figures of artists to the community of saints in the Church, wherein each saint represents a special trait symbolized by an attribute. In this pantheon, Van Gogh has the status of a Peter or a Christ.

It is he more than other figures that Fafard places in the ambiguous territory between painting and sculpture. It is here in the zone of betwixt and between, almost between spirit and flesh, that Van Gogh's visionary otherness is declared. Never is he represented as completely human. More mortal figures are allowed to retain their roundness and corporeality. They are portrayed as men, Monet in robust middle age, Renoir as a frail, restless old man with arthritis-crippled hands. In *Dear Vincent*, Van Gogh's apotheosis is complete, his attributes of palette, brushes, luminous paint and lighted candle signifying art, faith, charity and the fleetingness of human life. Yet there is a sense in which the role of all of Fafard's figures is the same. Born of the reverie that imagines while it remembers, they connect the past to the present, as surely as the funerary statues of Ancient Egypt do, declaring that indeed the past is real.

12. Umberto Eco, *Art and Beauty in the Middle Ages*, trans. Hugh Bredin (New Haven and London: Yale University Press, 1986), p. 66.

Artists and Other Figures

2
Dear Vincent

1983/1984
Bronze, patinated, 1/7
63.9 x 27.3 x 39.9 cm
Private collection

3
Dear Vincent

1983/1986
Bronze, patinated and painted, 6/7
63 x 28 x 41 cm
Kenneth Dushinski, Lakewood, Colorado

1
Dear Vincent

1983
Clay, painted
63.5 x 28 x 44 cm
Collection of the artist

5
VINCENT
1982
Clay
101.5 x 68 x 23 cm
Collection of the artist

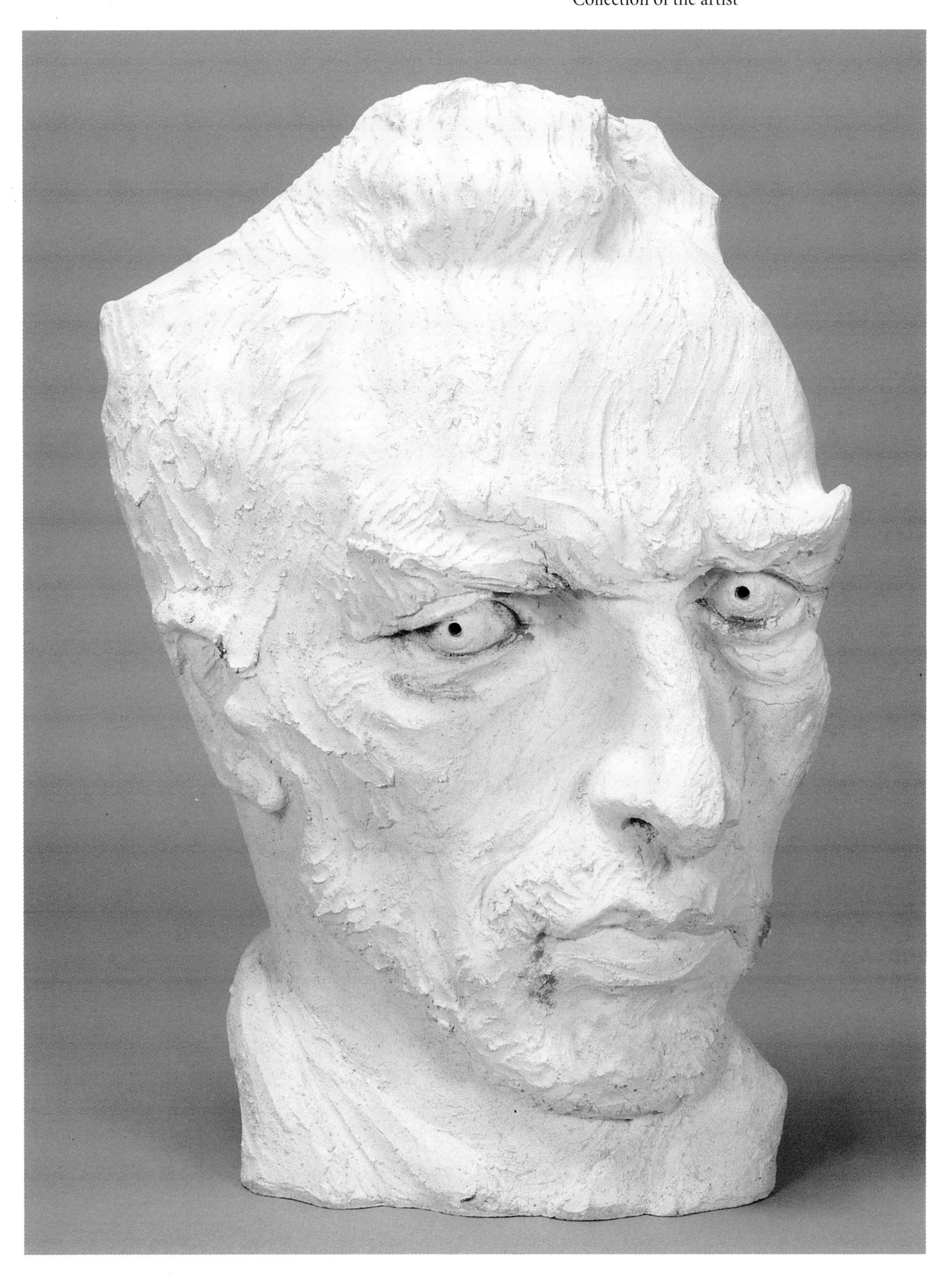

4
VINCENT NO. 4
1982
Clay, painted
77 x 45 x 60 cm
Canadian Broadcasting
Corporation, Regina

7
WOUNDED VINCENT
1982/1994
Bronze, patinated, 2/7
75 x 60 x 22 cm
Courtesy Mira Godard Gallery

6
Vincent

1982/1986
Bronze, patinated and painted, a.p.
99.7 x 68.5 x 19.2 cm
Mendel Art Gallery, Saskatoon; 87.26

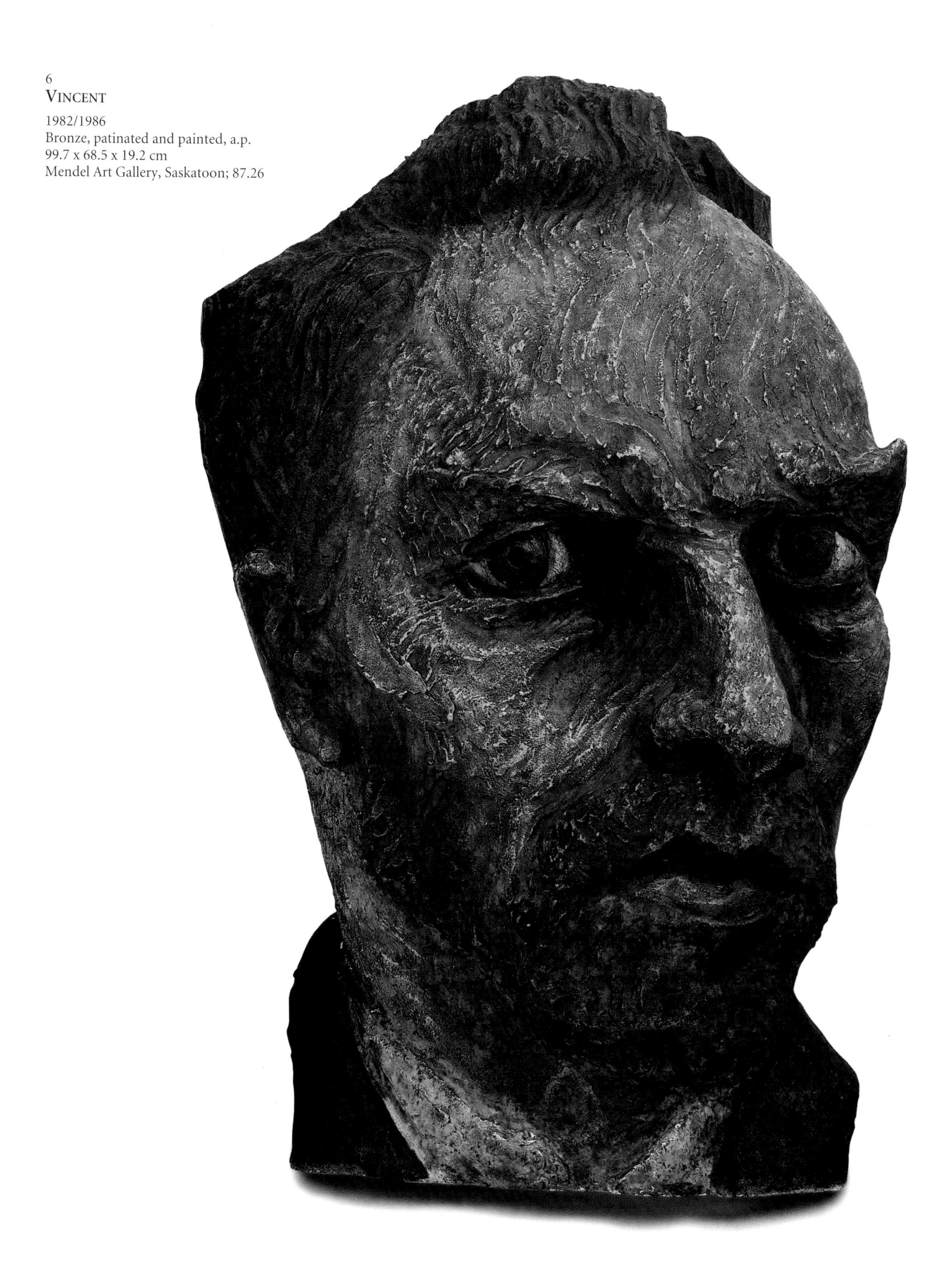

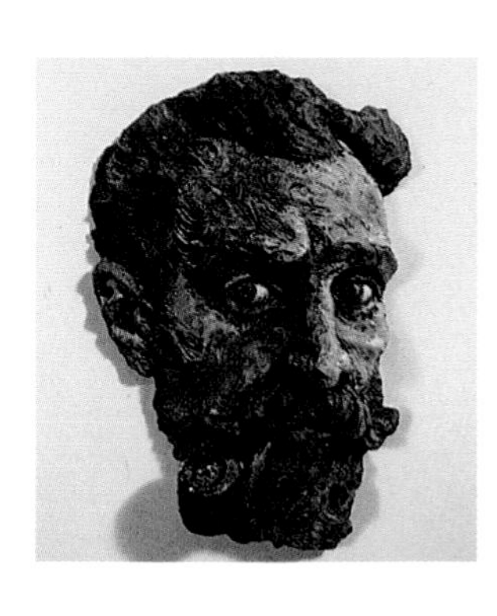
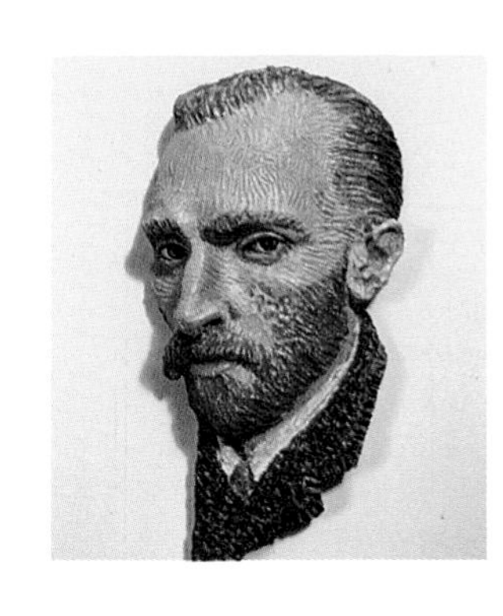

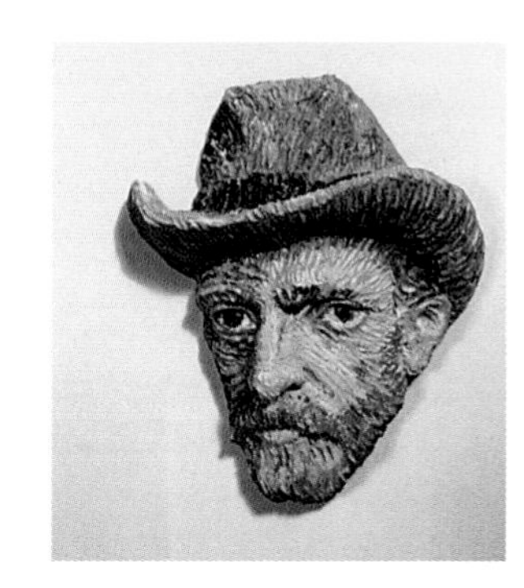
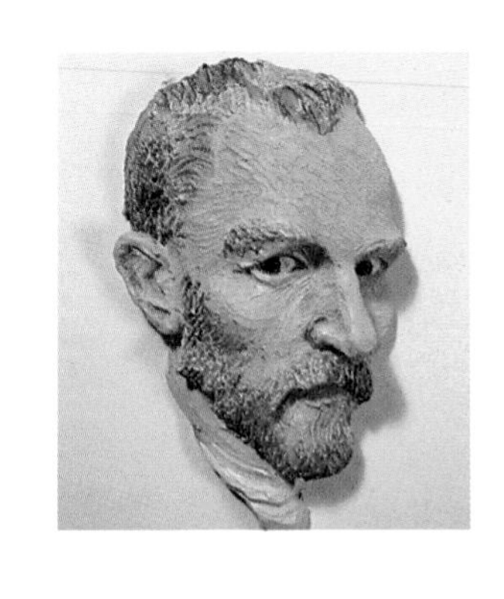
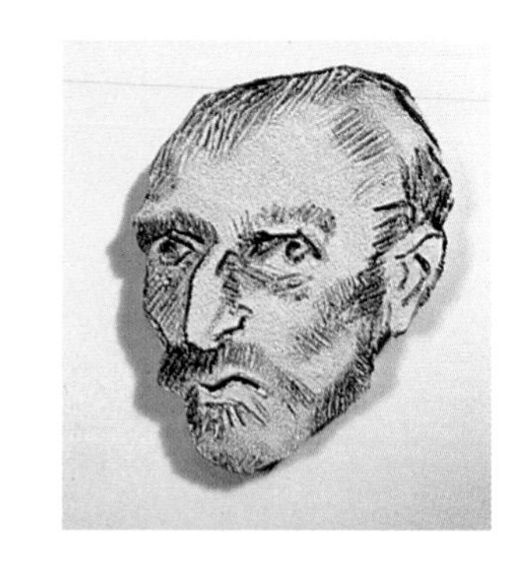
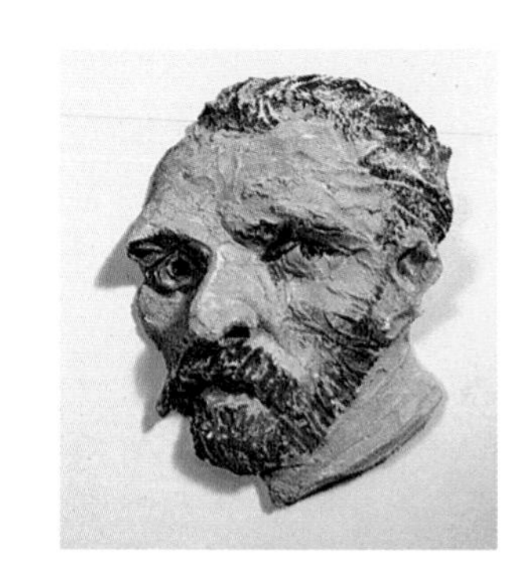
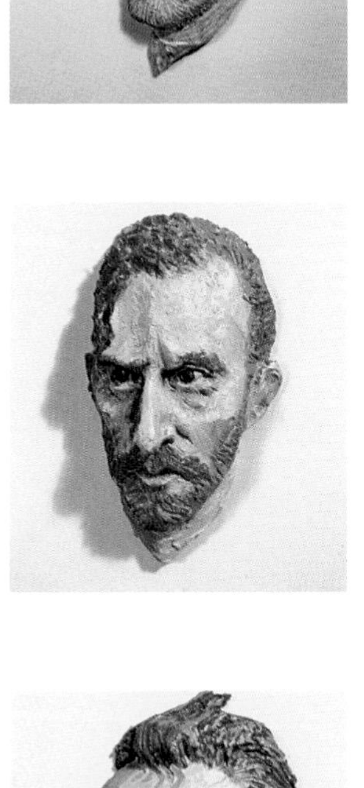
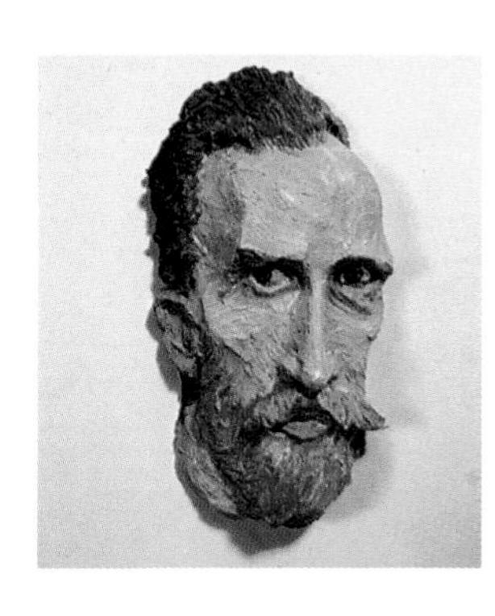
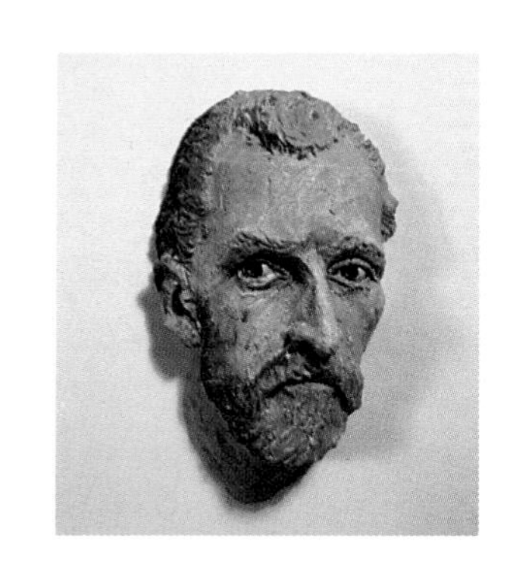
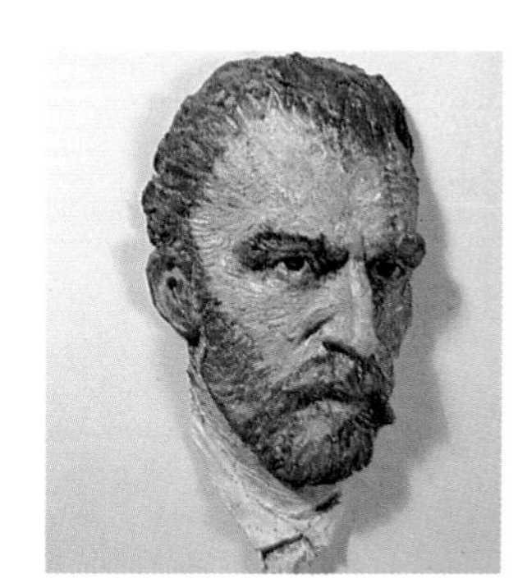

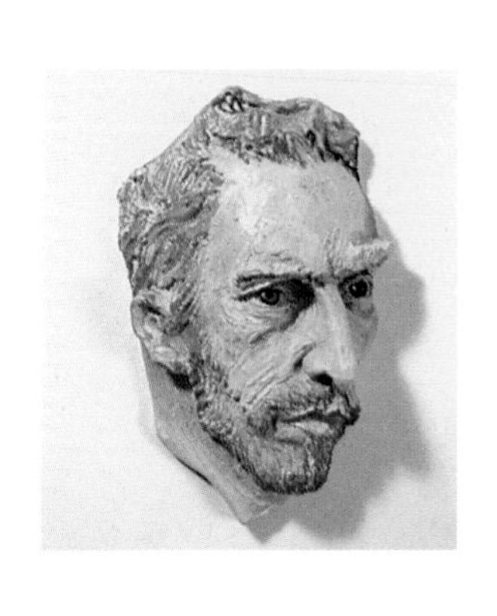
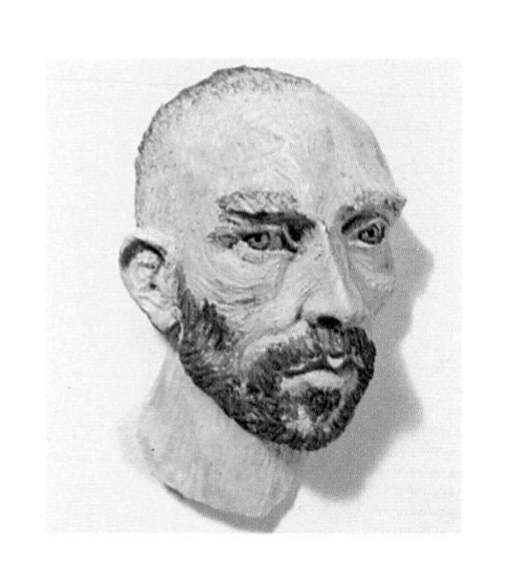
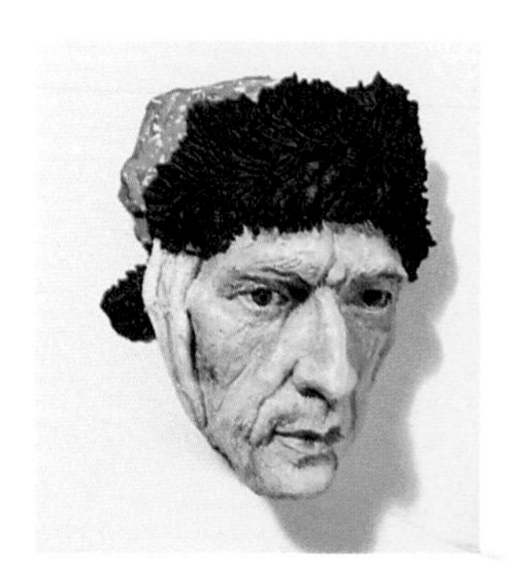

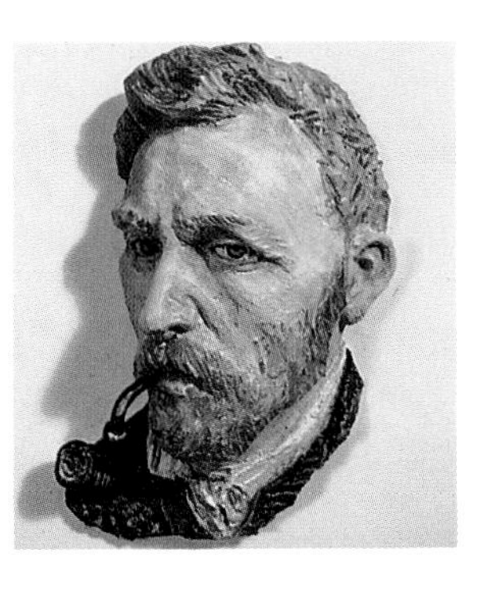

8
VINCENT SELF-PORTRAIT SERIES

1982-1983/1987
Clay, painted,
40 relief heads
Approx.
25 x 17 x 6.5 cm each
Margaret R. Odishaw
and Dr. Edmond
Charleton

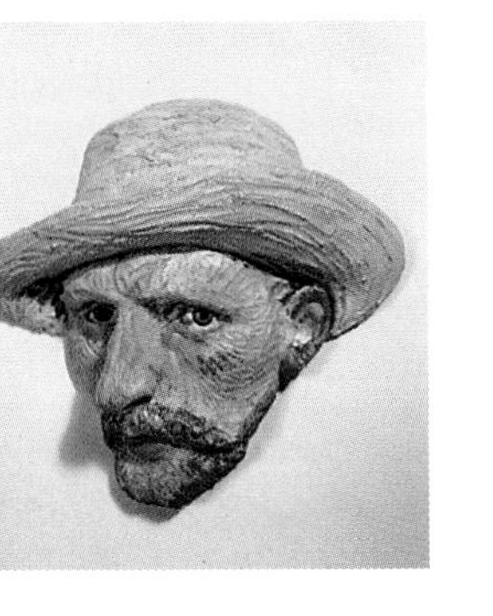

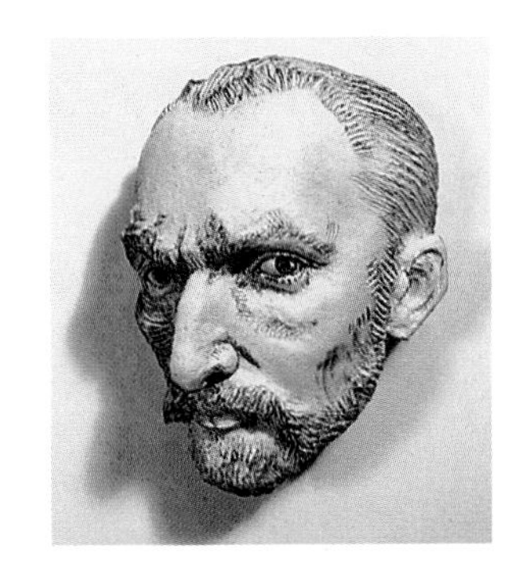
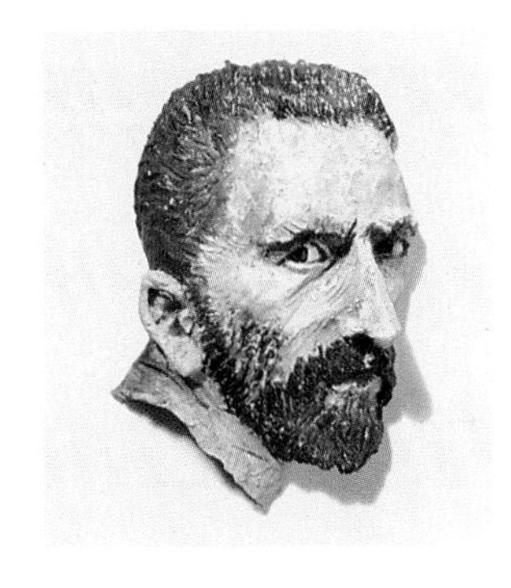
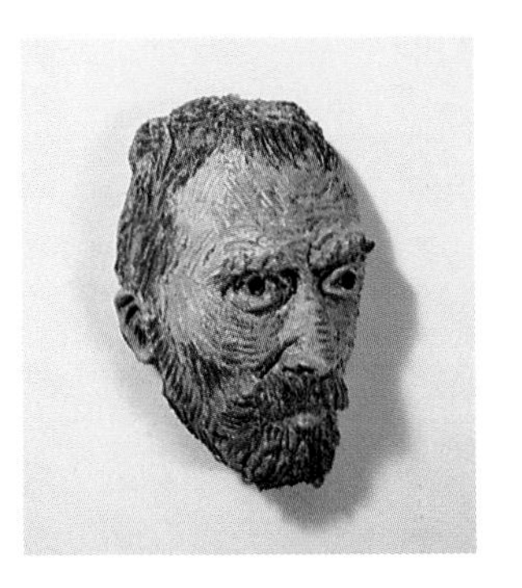
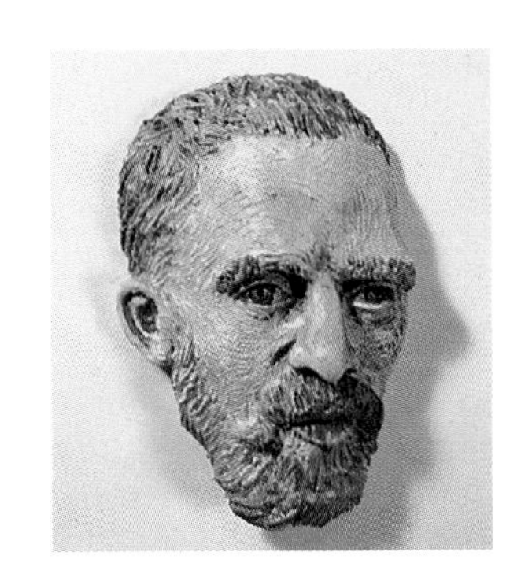

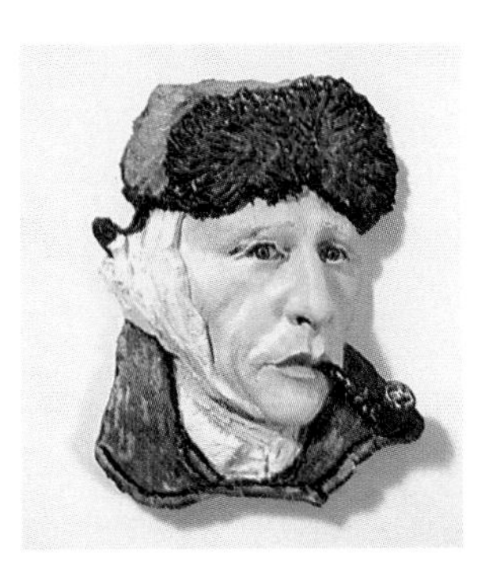
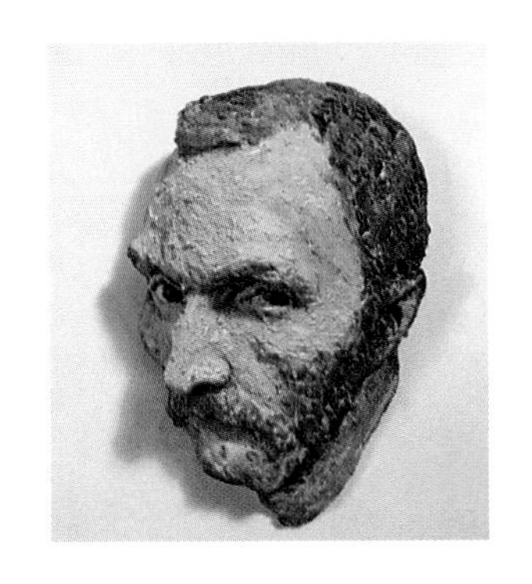

10
VINCENT ULTIMO

1982/1994
Bronze, patinated, 1/7
95 x 61 x 19 cm
Private collection, courtesy Galerie Woltjen

9
VINCENT (JAPANESE)

1982
Clay, painted
75 x 58 x 23 cm
Roy Lacaud Heenan

12
WALKING THE DARK SIDE

1987/1991
Bronze, patinated, 2/7
31.6 x 14 x 14 cm
Karen Dushinski, Edmonton

13
CÉZANNE

1981
Clay, painted
88 x 56 x 23 cm
The National Gallery of Canada, Ottawa; 28117

11
THE PAINTER

1986
Bronze, patinated and painted; wood and
Arborite base, 1/7
64.7 x 53.3 x 22.8 cm (figure)
94 x 64 x 33 cm (base)
Garth H. Drabinsky collection, Toronto

15
CÉZANNE I
1986
Bronze, patinated and painted, 2/5
55.5 x 30 x 43.5 cm
Garth H. Drabinsky collection, Toronto

16
CÉZANNE II
1986
Bronze, patinated and painted, 1/7
58 x 30 x 26 cm
Sheelagh Cluney, London, England

14
CÉZANNE I
1986
Clay, painted; bronze, wool
56 x 30 x 47 cm
Private collection

17
CÉZANNE II

1986
Bronze, patinated and painted, 7/7
58.1 x 28.3 x 26.8 cm
Courtesy Douglas Udell Gallery

18
CÉZANNE III

1986
Bronze, patinated and painted, 2/7
32.5 x 16 x 13 cm
Gerald N. Pencer

20
LE PETIT DANSEUR
1988
Bronze, patinated, 1/5
57 x 26 x 16 cm
The Montreal Museum of Fine Arts;
purchase, Horsley and
Annie Townsend Bequest, 1989.5

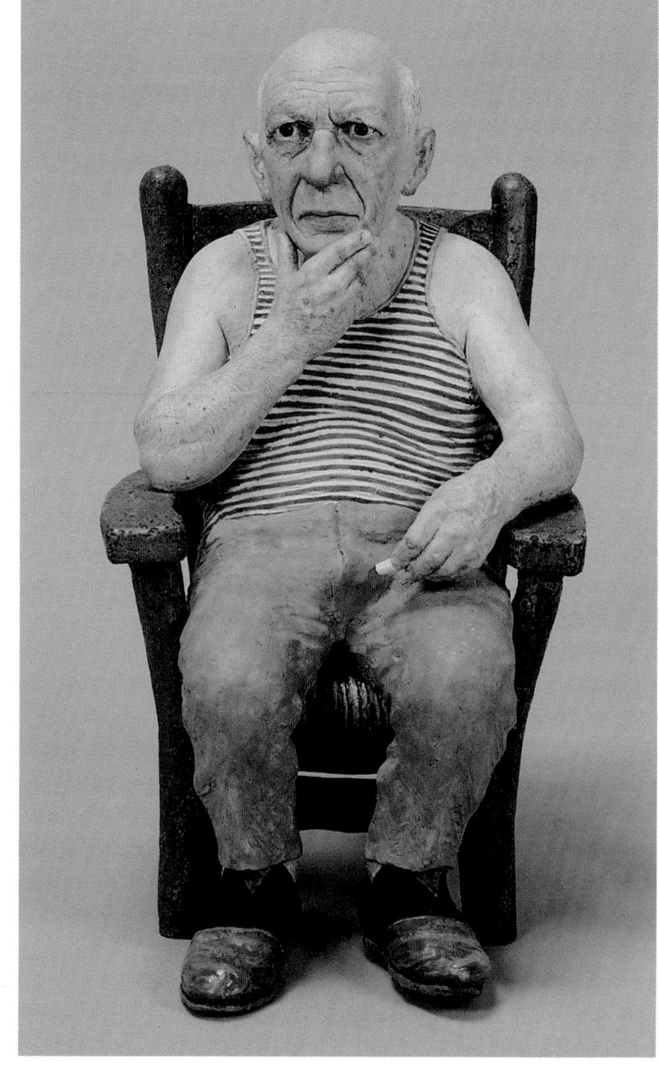

19
MY PICASSO
1981
Clay, glazed and painted
46.1 x 26.3 x 33.5 cm
Collection of the artist

21
Standing Pablo
1988
Clay, painted
74 x 39.9 x 33.4 cm
Collection of the artist

22
The Opening
1988
Bronze, patinated and painted; light, glass, 1/5
84 x 45.5 x 32 cm
Claridge Collection, Montreal

23
LE DOUANIER

1989
Bronze, patinated and painted, 7/7
29.5 x 19 x 22 cm
Private collection

26
MONET

1993
Bronze, patinated, 2/5
66 x 30.5 x 22.9 cm
Courtesy Mira Godard Gallery

24
Auguste

1993
Bronze, patinated and painted, a.p.
55.9 x 30.5 x 25.4 cm
Private collection

25
Renoir

1993
Bronze, patinated and painted, 3/5
56 x 21.5 x 38 cm
Richard and Catherine Fraser

27
Manitoba

1988 (after a clay version of 1975)
Bronze, patinated, 4/5
33 x 67 x 20 cm
Winnipeg Art Gallery; acquired with funds from The Winnipeg Foundation and from The Royal Canadian Academy of Art, G-88-424

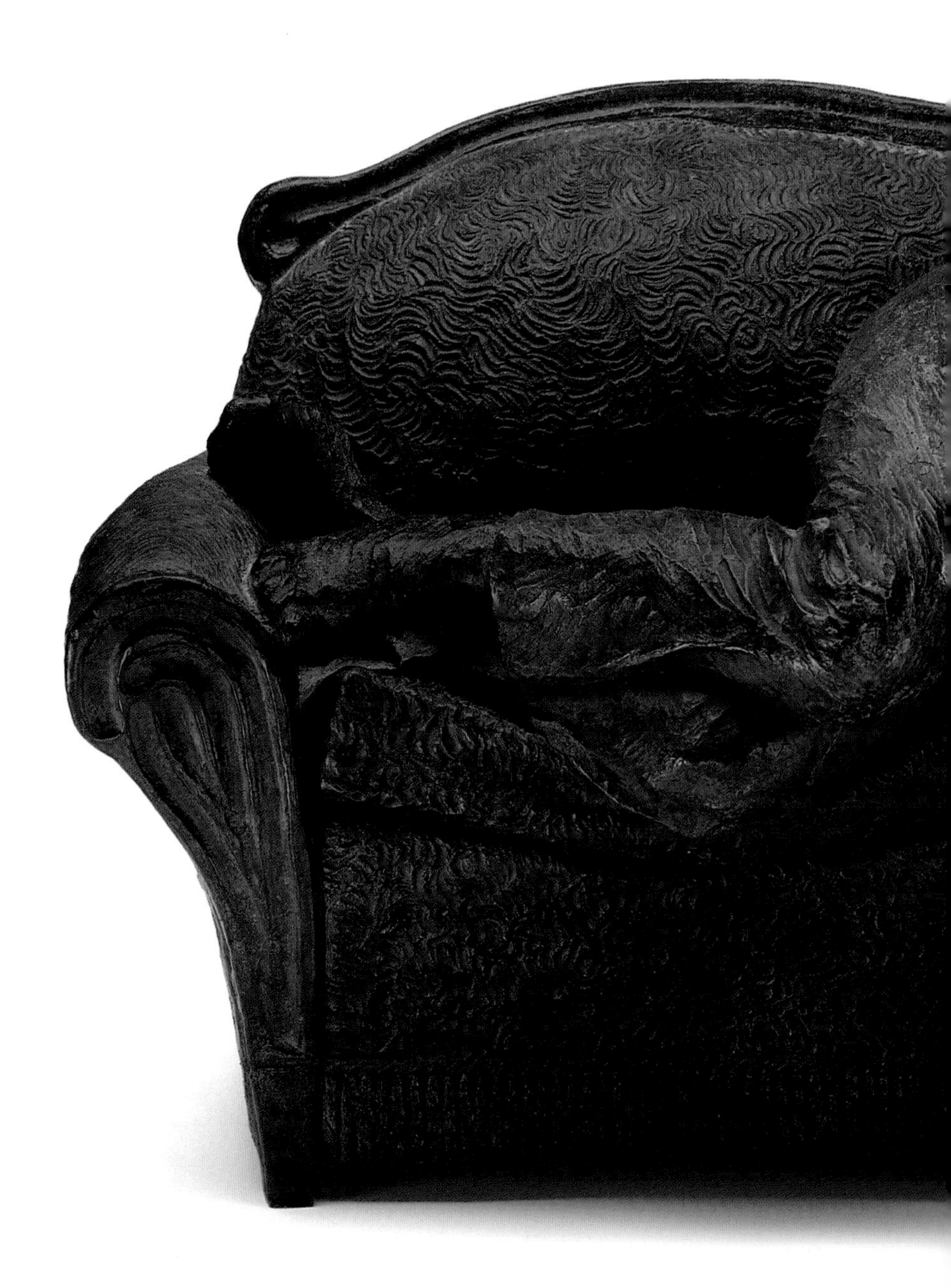

28
ASLEEP IN HIS MOTHER'S HOUSE
1988
Bronze, patinated and painted, 3/7
14 x 27.8 x 18.7 cm
Brenda and David McLean

29
THE INVENTOR ON HIS INVENTION
1988
Bronze, patinated and painted, 4/5
33.2 x 67 x 38 cm
The Montreal Museum of Fine Arts; purchase, gift of the Gelmont Foundation, 1995.24

30
The Terrorized

1988
Bronze, patinated, 1/5
83 x 35 x 29.5 cm
Courtesy Douglas Udell Gallery

31
CORTEZ
1988/1991
Bronze, patinated, 1/5
69.5 x 51 x 42 cm
Collection of the artist

32
JOAN OF ARC
1990
Bronze, polished and patinated, 1/5
57.5 x 64 x 24.5 cm
Private collection

33
The Evil Moon Guides the Santa Maria to the New World

1990
Bronze, patinated, 2/5
108.5 x 63 x 43 cm
Courtesy Douglas Udell Gallery

Cattle and Horses

34
The Pasture

1984-1985
Bronze, patinated, 7 units
140 x 290 x 150 cm each
The Cadillac Fairview Corporation Limited,
The Toronto Dominion Bank and the
Toronto-Dominion Centre West

35
Foreshortened Standing Cow
1985/1986
Bronze, patinated, 5/9
30 x 26 x 18 cm
Terry and Michele Veeman

36
Régine
1986
Bronze, patinated, 1/5
42 x 39.5 x 31.5 cm
Private collection

37
Manfighter
1986
Bronze, patinated, 1/1
38 x 15 x 35 cm
Joseph and Zhenia Maslany, Regina

38
Taureau
1986
Bronze, patinated, 5/5
46 x 48 x 46 cm
Bob and Lasha Roche collection

39

Smoothly She Shifted

1986/1987, repatinated 1996
Bronze, patinated, 1/2
113 x 114.2 x 51 cm
Courtesy Mira Godard Gallery

40

Assyrian Cows

1987
Bronze, patinated, 5 units, 1-5/5
51.3 x 29.3 x 5.1 cm each
Private collection

41
Lascaux
1988
Bronze, patinated, 1/5
71.5 x 65 x 28 cm
Carol and J. R. Shaw

42
Arthur
1988
Bronze, patinated, 1/5
68 x 63.5 x 33.3 cm
Private collection

43
ALBERT AND VICTORIA

1988
Bronze, patinated, 5/5
41 x 53 x 36 cm
Private collection, courtesy
Douglas Udell Gallery

44
Princess Louise

1988/1989
Bronze, patinated, 2/5
140.3 x 67.5 x 35 cm
The Montreal Museum of Fine Arts; purchase,
Horsley and Annie Townsend Bequest, 1989.6

45
VUILLARD

1989
Bronze, patinated, 5/5
26 x 64.8 x 39.4 cm
Veronica and David Thauberger collection

46
VUILLARD

1989/1995
Bronze, patinated, a.p.
26.5 x 65 x 40 cm
Edie and Barrie Cubbon collection

47
Snow

1989
Bronze, patinated, 5/5
80.2 x 32.6 x 16.2 cm
Private collection

48
Elinore

1989, repatinated 1996
Bronze, patinated, 2/5
53.3 x 128.3 x 53.4 cm
Mira Godard and Reg Bennett collection

49
Géricault

1990
Bronze, patinated, 1/1
50 x 50 x 20 cm
Private collection

50
Potter

1990, repatinated 1996
Bronze, patinated, 1/5
54.9 x 137.8 x 80 cm
Mira Godard and Reg Bennett collection

51
Valadon

1990, repatinated 1996
Bronze, patinated, 1/5
94 x 140 x 43.1 cm
Mira Godard and Reg Bennett collection

53
Altamira I
1991
Bronze, patinated, 1/1
61 x 48 x 20 cm
Cam Allard

52
TOPIARY

1991
Bronze, patinated, 1/1
96 x 61 x 46 cm
Cam Allard

54
GRIS

1991
Bronze, patinated, 3/3
154.9 x 81.3 x 76.2 cm
Private collection

55
Vie en Vie

1991
Bronze, patinated, 2/3
195.6 x 203.2 x 119.4 cm
Jane and Raphael Bernstein; S.932

56
Vie en Vie I

1991, repatinated 1996
Bronze, patinated, 1/1
66 x 75 x 33 cm
Courtesy Susan Whitney Gallery

57
Bosseur
1991
Bronze, patinated, 1/3
190.5 x 254 x 106.7 cm
Norman and Dixie Jewison

58
Teevo's Mom

1991-1992, repatinated in 1995
Bronze, patinated, 5/5
24 x 63 x 31 cm
Collection of the artist

59
Teevo

1993
Bronze, patinated, 2/5
70 x 90 x 42 cm
Private collection

60
AYRSHIRE
1993
Bronze, patinated, 4/5
30.5 x 66 x 48.3 cm
Courtesy Susan Whitney Gallery

61
AYRSHIRE
1993
Bronze, patinated, 5/5
30.5 x 66 x 48.3 cm
Gordon R. Diamond, Vancouver

62
Chicoute

1994
Bronze, patinated, 1/5
71.1 x 83.8 x 15.2 cm
Courtesy Ann and Roger Phillips, Regina

63
Zeta

1995
Bronze, patinated, 1/1
215.5 x 166 x 112 cm
Louise and Bernard Lamarre

64
Girt

1988
Bronze, patinated, 6/12
24.2 x 30.5 x 7.5 cm
Private collection

66
Albrecht

1990
Bronze, patinated, 4/5
51 x 59 x 20 cm
Private collection

65
Uccello

1989
Bronze, patinated, 1/5
87 x 89 x 28 cm
Private collection

67
Too-in-Wan

1994
Bronze, patinated, 1/1
62 x 79 x 13 cm
Private collection

68
Chloé

1994
Bronze, patinated, 1/1
160 x 137 x 68.5 cm
Courtesy Douglas Udell Gallery

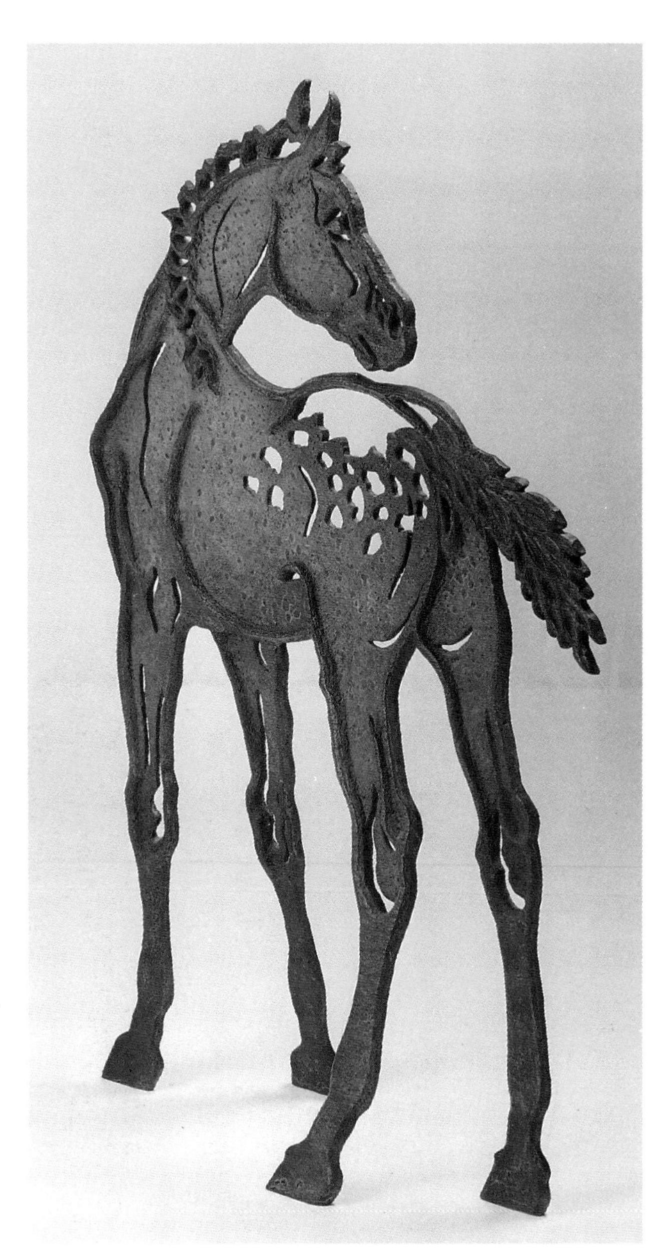

69
Jori
1994
Bronze, patinated, 1/1
57 x 40 x 17 cm
Ken and Karen Powell collection

70
Kiran
1994
Bronze, patinated, 1/1
129.5 x 86.4 x 38.1 cm
Courtesy Trépanier Baer Gallery, Calgary

71
Sandhya

1994
Bronze, patinated, 1/1
133.4 x 68.6 x 30.5 cm
Courtesy Trépanier Baer Gallery, Calgary

72
Cheyanne

1994
Bronze, patinated, 1/1
128.3 x 87.6 x 38.1
Private collection

75
Arti
1994
Bronze, patinated, 1/1
129.5 x 94 x 30.5 cm
Courtesy Trépanier Baer Gallery, Calgary

74
Guddi
1994
Bronze, patinated, 1/1
128.3 x 71.1 x 33 cm
Dr. Eunice Janzen collection, Saskatoon

73
Meena

1994
Bronze, patinated, 1/1
129.5 x 86.4 x 33 cm
David and Marie Kaufman collection

76
Hamish

1994/1995
Bronze, patinated, 4/5
59 x 68 x 24 cm
Dr. and Mrs. Zelick Perler

Tables

78
Boxer Table

1986
Bronze, patinated; glass, 1/2
39.5 x 77 x 77 cm (bronze)
Roy Lacaud Heenan

77
Calf Table

1986
Bronze, patinated, 1/3
109 x 58 x 29.5 cm
Private collection

79
Morris
1987
Bronze, patinated; glass, 1/1
85 x 34 x 34 cm (bronze)
Private collection

80
Morris Sonorous
1988
Bronze, patinated; glass, 3/4
84.5 x 71.3 x 42 cm (bronze)
A. E. MacLennan

81
Morris and Eve
1988/1995
Bronze, patinated; cast glass, 3/4
96.5 x 43.2 x 43.2 cm
Courtesy Trépanier Baer Gallery, Calgary

82
Minuet Minuit

1988
Bronze, patinated; glass, 1/1
44.5 x 81 x 55 cm (bronze)
Private collection

83
Bull Moose

1989
Bronze, patinated, a.p.
135.4 x 49.8 x 42.4 cm
Laurentian University Museum and Art Centre,
Sudbury, Ontario

84
Reindeer Table

1991/1995
Bronze, patinated, 1/5
84.5 x 75 x 38 cm
Courtesy Susan Whitney Gallery

85
Fox Table

1991
Bronze, patinated, 1/5
44.5 x 137.2 x 62.9 cm
Charles Russell, Edmonton

86
Explorer Table

1991
Bronze, patinated, 1/5
44 x 135 x 75 cm
Douglas Udell Gallery

87
Rendez-vous II

1992
Bronze, patinated; glass, 2/3
44 x 130 x 69 cm (bronze)
Private collection

88

Celtic Horse Table

1996
Bronze, patinated; glass, 1/5
73.7 x 63.5 x 74.5 cm (bronze)
Kim and Tony Allard

Cattle and Horses in Stainless Steel

89
ESCHER'S COW III

1993
Laser-cut steel, powder-coated, 1/3
116.5 x 163.5 x 41 cm
Douglas Udell Gallery

91
Clarisse I
1993
Stainless steel, painted, 7/10
13 x 15.5 cm
Collection of the artist

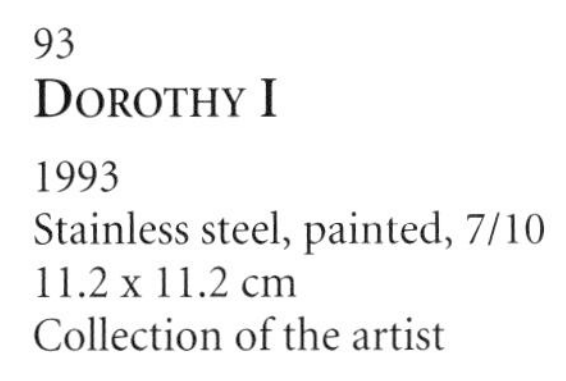

93
Dorothy I
1993
Stainless steel, painted, 7/10
11.2 x 11.2 cm
Collection of the artist

90
Andrea I
1993
Stainless steel, painted, 7/10
13 x 8.4 cm
Collection of the artist

92
Beverly I
1993
Stainless steel, painted, 7/10
11 x 10.2 cm
Collection of the artist

94
Enid I
1993
Stainless steel, painted, 7/10
11.5 x 8.6
Collection of the artist

95
Escher's Cow I
1993
Stainless steel, painted, 7/10
11.5 x 16.5 cm
Collection of the artist

98
Sonny Samson I
1993
Stainless steel, painted, 7/10
12.9 x 7.2 cm
Collection of the artist

96
Sam I
1993
Stainless steel, painted, 7/10
13.7 x 13 cm
Collection of the artist

97
Son of Samson
1993
Stainless steel, painted, 7/10
14 x 8.6 cm
Collection of the artist

101
Luke I

1994
Stainless steel, painted, 7/20
14.8 x 11.8 cm
Collection of the artist

99
Sasha I

1994
Stainless steel, painted, 7/20
17.5 x 10.2 cm
Collection of the artist

100
Chloé II

1994
Stainless steel, painted, 7/20
16.5 x 13 cm
Collection of the artist

103
Justin I

1994
Stainless steel, painted, 7/20
17.2 x 10.2 cm
Collection of the artist

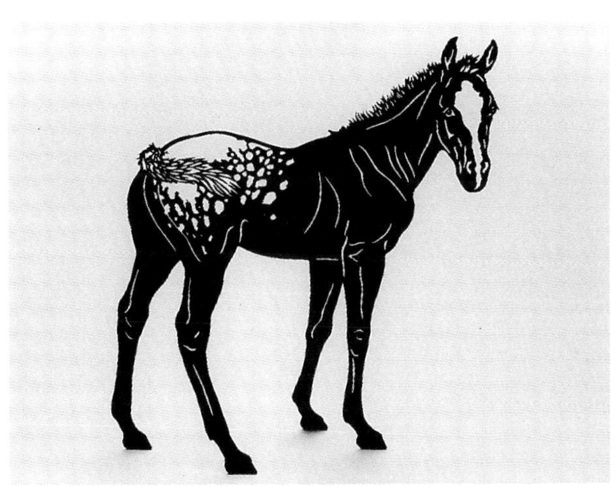

102
Mat I

1994
Stainless steel, painted, 7/20
14.3 x 13.4 cm
Collection of the artist

104
June II
1994
Stainless steel, painted, 7/20
12.4 x 14 cm
Collection of the artist

105
Potter II
1995
Stainless steel, painted, 7/20
9.5 x 20.3 x 4.5 cm
Collection of the artist

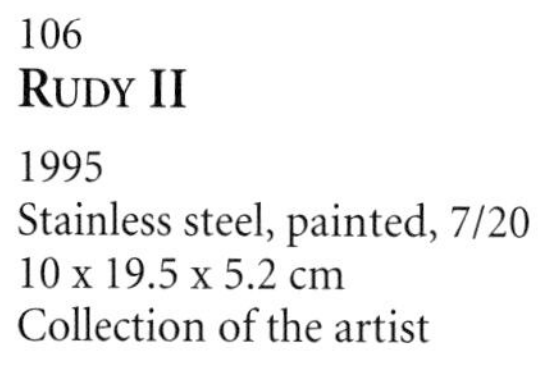

106
Rudy II
1995
Stainless steel, painted, 7/20
10 x 19.5 x 5.2 cm
Collection of the artist

107
Elka II
1995
Stainless steel, painted, 7/20
10.8 x 21 x 4 cm
Collection of the artist

108
Clarence II
1995
Stainless steel, painted, 7/20
17 x 10.7 cm
Collection of the artist

The Artist's Techniques

In this exhibition are presented sculptures by Joe Fafard, primarily from the years 1983 to 1995, a period of transition and fruitful production for the artist. It was in 1983 that Fafard first experimented with bronze, and when in 1984 he was invited to enter a competition for an important outdoor commission, the "bronze years" of Joe Fafard began.

Before

As a student at the University of Manitoba in Winnipeg in 1965, Joe Fafard created a life-size plaster female nude, which was exhibited at the Art Students' Club. (It was later discovered on the grounds of the legislature and carted off by the local police.) In 1970, while teaching at the University of Saskatchewan, Regina Campus, Fafard had his first solo exhibition, *Exhibition of Local Talent: Fafard & others*, which featured acerbic plaster portrayals of a number of his colleagues.

It was at the same time that Fafard observed the playful creations of his fellow teacher David Gilhooly, a ceramic artist from California, and he decided to try his hand at clay sculpture. He enjoyed the immediacy and plasticity of this medium. A sixty-centimetre ceramic relief bust of the Art Department's janitor, *Ali*, and a *Dead Cow* were among the sculptures Fafard exhibited at the Moose Jaw Art Gallery in the autumn of 1970. By 1973, he had created enough ceramic work for the Winnipeg Art Gallery to organize an entire exhibition, *Joe Fafard's Pensées*, which included sculptures of cows as well as numerous small clay figures of the inhabitants of Pense, the Saskatchewan village where Fafard then lived.

When the size of a sculpture warranted it, Fafard occasionally ventured to work in cement. With his art students, he erected a metre-and-a-half-tall cement bust of Norman MacKenzie in front of the art gallery in Regina. During the ten years following his departure from the university in 1974, Fafard worked primarily with clay, a medium that suited him for its ability to be quickly shaped; but he has declared, "I was never really a ceramicist."[1]

The Bronze Years

In June 1984, Joe Fafard was invited to participate in a major outdoor sculpture competition for downtown Toronto. One requirement for the winning piece was that it must be made of a durable, nonferrous material. Although Fafard was at that time well known for his ceramic sculptures, by 1983 he had "come to the end of my arrangement with ceramics somehow. I was reaching out to do more fantastic things, to get some charge, so it was natural that at that moment I switched over to bronze." He made some tentative experiments in bronze at the studio foundry of Saskatoon artist Bill Epp.

1. Except as otherwise noted, the artist is quoted from interviews with the author that took place on November 11, 1995, and June 18, 1996.

Fig. 1. *The Pasture*, 1984-1985 (cat. 34)

When short-listed for the competition, Fafard went in search of a foundry that could handle his large-scale project. He took several of his ceramic sculptures on a trip to Edmonton and Cochrane, Alberta, giving *Dear Vincent* (cat. 2) to one foundry and a big lying-down bull to another to cast. While this test showed that Edmonton's talented Paris-trained artisan Pierre Lheritier produced a superior product, Fafard was concerned about that foundry's financial stability. He was considering going to Kalispell, Montana, where there are a number of art foundries, when he received a call from Jack Harmon, who had got wind of the job. Harmon owned a Vancouver foundry specializing in big work. Following a trip there and his winning the competition, Fafard concluded an agreement to produce a group of seven somewhat larger than life-size bronze cows, entitled *The Pasture* (fig. 1), for the Toronto-Dominion Centre.

When Fafard made the full-scale model at the Vancouver foundry, in December 1984, he worked directly, without mechanically enlarging the small model he had brought with him. "Jack Harmon hadn't seen that before, it's not the way he would have done it. It was a good learning experience for me, to be in that situation. And it was also something very useful for later on when I opened up my own foundry."

To create the full-size cow model, Fafard cut thick sheets of Styrofoam with a saw, sandwiched them together and then shaped the surface using a steel brush until he had the basic form. He achieved the final details and texture by covering the entire surface with plaster. The foundry then cut this model into fourteen segments and made a mould from each. These were cast in bronze seven times apiece, and the seven sets of fourteen segments welded together to make seven complete cows. They were finished by die-grinding the seams, patinating and applying a protective coat of wax. Each cow measures almost three metres in length and weighs 540 kilograms on average. The deadline for installation was mid-October 1985, and it was met with only hours to spare.

The experience of working in and with the Vancouver foundry led Fafard to consider opening a foundry of his own in Pense, where he also had his studio. Fafard had sketched a design for one, but "then a building in Pense came up for sale and it was almost exactly like my design – only a little bigger – so I bought it".[2] Just after *The Pasture* was installed in Toronto, the first bronze was poured at Fafard's foundry, Julienne Atelier, Inc.

2. Meta Perry, "Fafard Casts His Own", *The Leader-Post* [Regina], March 4, 1986, p. B-13.

Key to establishing Julienne Atelier was to develop a team of able technicians. Fafard first brought in Pierre Lheritier, whose expertise was essential to the enterprise. Others were hired and trained in the skills required by the various stages of production. But the most fundamental ingredient was Fafard himself, the artist and the entrepreneur. Fafard's facility in modelling clay, which remained the basis of the bronzes, his artistic vision and his spirit of experimentation led to new forms and colours in bronze.

Fig. 2. China, *Elephant*, Chou dynasty (about 1129-249 B.C.), bronze, h: 21 cm Freer Gallery of Art, Washington

The Bronze Casting Process

Joe Fafard's bronze sculptures are made principally by the "lost-wax" process, which has been in use for thousands of years. It was used by Chinese artisans, whose cast bronze ritual vessels sometimes took the form of animals (fig. 2), as well as by Egyptians and Greeks, and was revived during the Renaissance.

With slight variations, the process went as follows: A model of an object (a vessel, a sculpture) is formed in wax over a clay core – if one is needed. Details may be carved or applied in relief (fig. 3). Wax vents, called sprues, are attached to the wax model, and the whole is covered with several coats of liquid clay, or slurry. Each coat is allowed to dry thoroughly to form a hard shell. When the model is fired (fig. 4), the wax melts and escapes through the sprues, while inside the hollow coat of clay is left the imprint of the original. Then, molten bronze is poured in, filling

Fig. 3. Fafard working on a wax model

Fig. 4. A cast coming out of the kiln at Julienne Atelier

Fig. 5. Molten bronze

the space left by the wax (figs. 5-7). Finally, the shell is chipped away, and the vents, now bronze, are removed.

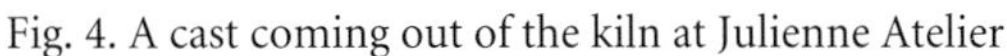

To make an edition of several bronze sculptures from the same model, as Fafard most often does, the casting process is basically the same, but the preparation of the model and mould is somewhat more involved. In this case, a preliminary model is made of plaster or clay which is fired. Damp clay is then applied in sheets about a centimetre thick over the entire surface. For stability, a heavy plaster "mother mould" is made to encase the original model and its damp coating of clay. Next, the mother mould is separated into two or more vertical sections, and the clay coating peeled from the original model. Fixed firmly to a base plaque, the model is then inserted back into the mother mould, and liquid rubber poured into the space formerly occupied by the damp clay coating. The rubber is catalyzed so that it hardens, the mother mould reopened, and the rubber layer removed. This rubber layer, which serves as a reusable mould, is then refitted into the mother mould and its interior thinly coated (approximately six millimetres) with melted wax (fig. 8). When the wax solidifies, the interior cavity is packed with a liquid mixture of plaster and brick granules, which is allowed to cure. The mother mould is finally opened for the third time and the rubber mould peeled off, leaving the desired wax model to be invested in slurry of brick and plaster that is poured around the wax model in a makeshift container formed with a casing of sheet metal.

Figs. 6-7. Bronze pouring

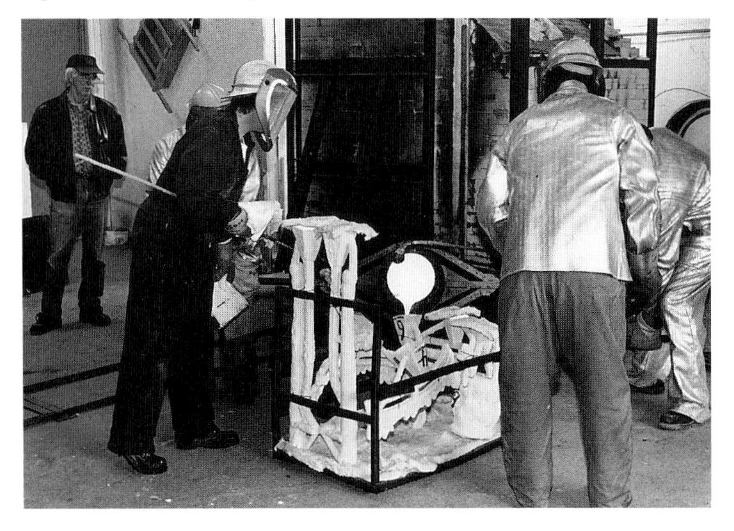

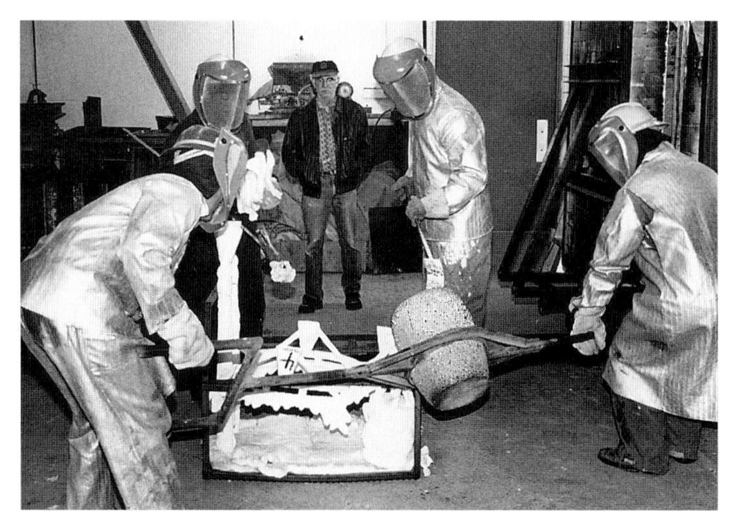

In recent years, the foundry has been converted from the brick and plaster mould method used to contain the poured molten bronze to the newer ceramic shell method that has been developed and used by industry over the past fifty years. This newer method is simpler. It is, in brief, a process where the wax is dipped in a special slurry and then in floating sand. Repeated coatings of slurry and sand form a tough shell which becomes ceramic-like during the firing in which the wax melts and is led off. Then the molten bronze is poured in.

Another process used by Fafard is sand casting. This involves creating a negative space in a bed of hard-packed sand, which has bottom and top layers – a sort of drawing in a sandwich. Molten bronze is poured in to fill up the voids. Bronze pieces produced in this manner are understandably unique. A variant of this process is "lost-Styrofoam" sand casting, in which carved Styrofoam linear forms are packed into the sand bed and are burned out and replaced by the hot liquid bronze. By using a master form from which the Styrofoam shapes are traced and cut, Fafard is able to reproduce several versions of the resulting bronze piece.

Fig. 8. A technician pouring wax

The last stage in preparing Fafard's bronze sculptures involves the addition of colour through patination. Patinas are the result of a chemical reaction with the metal. Nitric oxide, for instance, produces a green coloration; zinc oxide produces a white that can be stained with other compounds. Although Fafard is intrigued by the growing range of colour his technicians have achieved and encourages experimentation, he himself enjoys the role of artist-director.

After

In 1993, it was again an important sculpture competition that prompted Fafard to explore a new material. His proposal, first realized as a laser-cut maquette, included eight panels of interwoven figurative passages to be created at full scale in plasma-cut steel. Although the project has not yet been carried out, the experience led Fafard to try smaller works in laser-cut steel, of which *Escher's Cow III* (fig. 9) is an early example. Most recently, Fafard has completed a painted stainless steel bull bison, *Paskwamostos*, commissioned for Shaw Court in Calgary. However, "I still see potential in bronze. Learning a new technique is like learning a new word. There are certain limitations to this new technique that I wouldn't find completely satisfying. The idea is to have many different techniques."

Fig. 9. *Escher's Cow III*, 1993 (cat.89)

M. G.

JOSE

Joe Fafard with his technicians

JOE FAFARD was born September 2, 1942, in Sainte-Marthe, Saskatchewan.

He received a Bachelor of Fine Arts from the University of Manitoba, Winnipeg, in 1966, and a Master of Fine Arts from Pennsylvania State University in 1968. From 1968 to 1974, he was an instructor in sculpture at the University of Saskatchewan, Regina Campus. During the winter semester 1980-1981, he was visiting lecturer in sculpture at the University of California at Davis.

Joe Fafard was made an Officer of the Order of Canada in 1981. He received the Royal Architectural Institute of Canada Allied Arts Award in 1987 and an Honorary Doctorate from the University of Regina in 1989.

From 1971 to 1984, Fafard lived in Pense, Saskatchewan. In 1984, he moved to Regina, where he currently resides. In 1985, he opened a foundry, Julienne Atelier, Inc., in Pense.

Solo Exhibitions

1996
Vancouver, Douglas Udell Gallery, April 27 - May 11, 1996, *Joe Fafard*
Calgary, Trépanier Baer Gallery, June 13 - July 20, 1996, *Joe Fafard/Plus: New Works* (pamphlet)
Toronto, Mira Godard Gallery, October 19 - November 2, 1996, *Joe Fafard*

1995
Mississauga, Ontario, Mississauga Civic Centre, August - September 10, 1995
Regina, Susan Whitney Gallery, November 10 - December 5, 1995, *Joe Fafard: From the Domestic to the Majestic*

1994
Calgary, Trépanier Baer Gallery, February 17 - March 31, 1994, *Joe Fafard: The Horse Show*
Edmonton, Douglas Udell Gallery, May 30 - June 11, 1994, *Joe Fafard: New Work*

1993
Toronto, Mira Godard Gallery, September 11 - October 2, 1993, *Joe Fafard*
Regina, Susan Whitney Gallery, November 5 - December 8, 1993, *Joe Fafard*

1992
New York, 49th Parallel, Gallery for Contemporary Canadian Art, January 11 - February 8, 1992, *Joe Fafard: Outlines*
Vancouver, Douglas Udell Gallery, November 28 - December 24, 1992, *Joe Fafard: New Work*

1991
Winnipeg, Gallery 454, April - May 31, 1991
Edmonton, Woltjen/Udell Gallery, May 11 - June 8, 1991, *Joe Fafard*
Regina, Susan Whitney Gallery, November 7 - December 3, 1991, *Joe Fafard*
Toronto, Mira Godard Gallery, November 30 - December 21, 1991

1990
Toronto, Mira Godard Gallery, April 28 - May 16, 1990, *Joe Fafard: Fête Champêtre*
Chicago, Neville-Sargent Gallery, October 12 - November 3, 1990, *Joe Fafard: Recent Bronze Sculptures*
Edmonton, Woltjen/Udell Gallery, November 15 - December 6, 1990

1989
Regina, Susan Whitney Gallery, April 21 - May 16, 1989, *Joe Fafard*
Edmonton, Woltjen/Udell Gallery, May 3-27, 1989, *Joe Fafard*

1988
Toronto, Mira Godard Gallery, September 14 - October 1, 1988, *Joe Fafard*

1987-1988
Saskatoon, Mendel Art Gallery, October 2 - November 15, 1987, and Regina, Dunlop Art Gallery, December 12, 1987 - January 17, 1988, *Joe Fafard: Cows and Other Luminaries, 1977-1987* (catalogue)

1987
Regina, Susan Whitney Gallery, April 16 - May 12, 1987, *Joe Fafard*
Vancouver, Woltjen/Udell Gallery, October 31 - November 21, 1987, *Joe Fafard*

1986-1987
Regina, Joe Moran Gallery, November 23, 1986 - January 5, 1987, *Fafard: Drawing in Sand*

1986
Edmonton, Woltjen/Udell Gallery, February 10 - March 1986, *Joe Fafard: New Bronze Cows*
Toronto, Gallery Moos, November 8-26, 1986, *Joe Fafard*

1985
Vancouver, Diane Farris Gallery, November 9-23, 1985, *Joe Fafard: A Survey*

1984
Regina, Susan Whitney Gallery, November 1-20, 1984, *Joe Fafard*

1983
Swift Current, Saskatchewan, R.C. Dahl National Exhibition Centre, February 3 - March 4, 1983, *Joe Fafard* (pamphlet)
Edmonton, Woltjen/Udell Gallery, May 28 - June 18, 1983, *Open Secrets*
Winnipeg, Brian Melnychenko Gallery, October 30 - November 18, 1983, *Joe Fafard* (paintings)

1982
Winnipeg, Thomas Gallery, March 21 - April 17, 1982, *Joe Fafard*
Montreal, Galerie Don Stewart, March 27 - April 14, 1982, *Joe Fafard*
Regina, Susan Whitney Gallery, November 4-30, 1982, *Joe Fafard*

1981
Toronto, Gallery Moos, April 11-30, 1981, *Joe Fafard (and...)*, (pamphlet)

1980
Folsom, California, The Candy Store Gallery, April 6-30, 1980, *Joe Fafard*
Edmonton, Downstairs Gallery, October 30 - November 8, 1980, *Joe Fafard: Daisy I and Her Embryo Transplants*
Regina, Susan Whitney Gallery, November 13 - December 3, 1980, *Joe Fafard*

1979-1981
Edmonton, The Edmonton Art Gallery, September 7 - October 21, 1979 (travelled to Calgary, Saskatoon, Surrey, Lethbridge, Kingston, Hamilton, Banff, Oshawa, Charlottetown, Regina and Medicine Hat, to March 1981), *Joe Fafard: Recent Sculpture* (catalogue)

1979
Regina, Kesik Gallery, May 15 - June 2, 1979, *Joe Fafard*
Edmonton, Downstairs Gallery, November 19 - December 1, 1979, *Joe Fafard*

1977
Winnipeg, Thomas Gallery, March 18 - April 2, 1977, *Joe Fafard*
Edmonton, Downstairs Gallery, October 24 - November 5, 1977, *Joe Fafard*

1975
Pense, Saskatchewan, Town Hall, October 5, 1975, *Joe Fafard*

1974
Mississauga, Ontario, Sheridan Gallery, Sheridan College School of Design, November 4-20, 1974, *Joe Fafard*

1973
Saskatoon, Shoestring Gallery, January 1973
Edmonton, University of Alberta Art Gallery and Museum, February 14-18, 1973, *Joe Fafard* (poster)
Winnipeg, The Winnipeg Art Gallery, June 15 - July 30; Calgary, The Glenbow-Alberta Gallery, September 1-30; Vancouver, Vancouver Art Gallery, October-November; Regina, Dunlop Art Gallery, December 1-30, 1973, *Joe Fafard's Pensées* (catalogue)

1972
Calgary, Alberta College of Art Gallery, March 22 - April 3, 1972, *Joe Fafard: Ceramic Pictures* (pamphlet)

1971
Davis, California, Davis Art Centre, July 17 - August 7, 1971, *Joe Fafard*

1970
Regina, Dunlop Art Gallery, April 1-24, 1970, *Exhibition of Local Talent: Fafard & others*

SELECTED GROUP EXHIBITIONS

1995
Montreal, Old Port of Montreal, June 15 - September 17, 1995, *Skulptura Montréal 95* (catalogue)

1987-1988
Stockton, California, University of the Pacific Gallery, November 18 - December 10, 1987, and San Francisco, San Francisco State University Gallery, January 15 - February 15, 1988, *True North* (catalogue *True North/Far West*)

1984
Calgary, Alberta College of Art Gallery, June 21 - July 28, 1984, *3rd Annual Wild West Show* (catalogue)

1983
London, England, Canada House, April 20 - May 31, 1983 (travelled to Paris, Centre culturel canadien; Brussels, Centre culturel canadien), *5 Artistes de la Saskatchewan* (catalogue)

1982
London, Ontario, London Regional Art Gallery, May 21 - July 4, 1982, *Vic Cicansky/ Joe Fafard* (pamphlet)

1980
Ottawa, The National Gallery of Canada, July 5 - September 7, 1980, *Pluralities 1980/ Pluralités 1980* (catalogue)
Regina, Norman Mackenzie Art Gallery, University of Regina, September 12 - October 19, 1980, *The Continental Clay Connection* (catalogue)

1978-1979
Edmonton, The Edmonton Art Gallery, June 3-29, 1978 (travelled to Calgary, Glenbow-Alberta Institute, July 7 - August 30; Saskatoon, Mendel Art Gallery, September 15 - October 31; Windsor, Art Gallery of Windsor, November 12 - December 31, 1978; Hamilton, Art Gallery of Hamilton, February 15 - March 15, 1979; London, London Regional Art Gallery, May 15 - June 15; Saint John's, Memorial University of Newfoundland, July 1-30, 1979), *Certain Traditions: Recent British and Canadian Art* (catalogue)

1978
Regina, Norman Mackenzie Art Gallery, April 29 - May 28, 1978, *Regina: 25 Years, 1953-1978* (catalogue)

1976
Halifax, Dalhousie University Art Gallery, August 2 - September 7, 1976, *Messages from Southern Saskatchewan* (catalogue)
Calgary, Glenbow-Alberta Institute, September 22 - October 24, 1976, *Western Untitled* (catalogue)

1974
Montreal, Espace 5, April 17 - May 5, 1974, *Céramiques de Victor Cicansky, Joe Fafard, David Gilhooly*
Victoria, The Art Gallery of Greater Victoria, October 29 -November 24, 1974, *Fired Sculpture* (catalogue)

1973
Toronto, Art Gallery of Ontario, March 29 - April 23, 1973, and New York, New York Cultural Centre, June 15 - July 20, 1973, *Ceramic Objects* (pamphlet)
Paris, Musée d'Art moderne de la Ville de Paris, June 14 - August 15, 1973, *Canada Trajectoires 73* (catalogue)
Kanazawa City, Japan, August 18 - October 14, 1973, *The Sensible Cup International Exhibition* (catalogue)

1972
Kingston, Ontario, Agnes Etherington Art Centre, Queen's University, September 19 - October 22, 1972, *Realism: Emulsion and Omission* (catalogue)
Los Angeles, David Stuart Galleries, October 3 - October 28, 1972, *The Cup Show*

1970-1971
Kitchener, Kitchener-Waterloo Art Gallery, September 11 - October 4, 1970 (circulated by the Art Gallery of Ontario, Toronto, to July 1971) *Saskatchewan: Saskatoon and Regina* (catalogue)

1970
Montreal, The Montreal Museum of Fine Arts, May 8 - June 7, and Toronto, Art Gallery of Ontario, August 7 - September 6, 1970, *Survey/Sondage 70: Realism(e)s* (pamphlet)
Burnaby, British Columbia, Burnaby Art Gallery, October 1-30, 1970, *Gilhooly, Fafard, Thauberger: Funk 3*
Moose Jaw, Saskatchewan, Moose Jaw Art Gallery, November 17 - December 6, 1970, *Joe Fafard and Bev Kelly*

Selected Bibliography

Alberta College of Art Gallery. *Joe Fafard: Ceramic Pictures*, exhib. pamphlet. Text by David Zack. Calgary, 1972. 8 pp.

Bodolai, Joe. "Masters of Naïve Art. Joe Fafard: One Man's Private Prairie Album". *Saturday Night*, vol. 90, no. 6 (November 1975), pp. 30-31.

Edmonton Art Gallery. *Joe Fafard: Recent Sculpture*, exhib. cat. Text by Terrence Heath. Edmonton, 1979. 22 pp.

Enright, Robert. "Working in the Flatland: An Interview with Joe Fafard", *Border Crossings*, vol. 7, no.1 (January 1988), pp.10-20.

Fafard, Joe, documentation by Eberhard Otto. "Joe Fafard". *Artscanada*, vol. 29, no. 2 (Spring 1972), pp. 14-19.

———. "The Pasture: A Proposal to Bring Cows to Downtown Toronto". *Brick*, no. 25 (Fall 1985), pp. 28-29.

Gallery Moos. *Joe Fafard (and...)*, exhib. pamphlet. Text by Patrick Lane and Lorna Uher. Toronto, 1981.

Heath, Terrence. "The Regina Ceramists". *Artscanada*, vol. 30, no. 2 (May 1973), p. 68.

———. "The Figure of Fafard". *Brick*, no. 25 (Fall 1985), pp. 26-27.

———. "The Accessible Innovator". *Border Crossings*, vol. 9, no. 3 (July 1990), pp.25-26.

London Regional Art Gallery. *Vic Cicansky/Joe Fafard*, exhib. pamphlet. Text by Mayo Graham. London, Ontario, 1982. 10 pp.

Mandel, Eli. "A Comprehensible World: The Work of Cicansky, Thauberger, Yuristy and Fafard" (includes statements by the artists). *Artscanada*, vol. 36, no. 3 (October-November 1979), pp. 15-19.

Mays, John Bentley. "Things Are Looking Up for Public Art". *The Globe and Mail* [Toronto], November 23, 1985, p. D-17.

McConathy, Dale. "The Artist's Image of Himself" (statements by various artists). *Artscanada*, vol. 32, no. 3 (Autumn 1975), pp. 50-54.

McConnell, Clyde S. "Two Regina Artists: Fafard and Lambert-Kelly". *Artscanada*, vol. 27, no. 5 (October-November 1970), pp. 79-80.

The National Gallery of Canada. *Pluralities 1980/Pluralités 1980*, exhib. cat. Text by Philip Fry. Ottawa 1980. Pp. 55-60.

Old Port of Montreal. *Skulptura Montréal 95: International Exhibition of Open Air Sculptures*, exhib. cat. Text by Léo Rosshandler. Montreal: Centre de diffusion 3D, 1995. Pp. 36-37.

Perry, Meta. "Fafard Casts His Own". *The Leader-Post* [Regina], March 4, 1986, p. B-13.

Shuebrook, Ron. "Regina Funk". *Art and Artists*, vol. 8, no. 5 (August 1973), pp. 38-41.

Teitelbaum, Matthew, and Peter White. *Joe Fafard: Cows and Other Luminaries, 1977-1987*, exhib. cat. Saskatoon: Mendel Art Gallery, 1987. 59 pp.

Tousley, Nancy. "Community Spirit". *Canadian Art*, vol. 5, no. 1 (Spring/March 1988), pp. 56-61.

Trépanier Baer Gallery, *Joe Fafard/Plus: New Works*, exhib. pamphlet. Text by Katherine Ylitalo. Calgary, 1996. 4 pp.

Winnipeg Art Gallery. *A Souvenir Album of Joe Fafard's Pensées*, exhib. cat. Text by Joe Fafard. Winnipeg, 1973. 16 pp.

Zack, David, "Fafard : critique déguisé en artiste". *Vie des Arts*, no. 64 (Autumn 1971), pp. 42-45 (in English on pp. 89-91).

Zwarun, Suzanne. "That Artist Fella". *Maclean's*, vol. 90, no. 15 (July 25, 1977), pp. 22-28.

Lenders to the Exhibition

The Montreal Museum of Fine Arts gratefully acknowledges the following institutions and individuals, whose loans have made this exhibition possible.

Cam Allard
Kim and Tony Allard
Jane and Raphael Bernstein
The Cadillac Fairview Corporation Limited,
  Toronto Dominion Bank and
  Toronto-Dominion Centre West, Toronto
Canadian Broadcasting Corporation, Regina
Dr. Edmond Charleton
Claridge Collection, Montreal
Sheelagh Cluney, London, England
Edie and Barrie Cubbon
Gordon R. Diamond, Vancouver
Douglas Udell Gallery
Garth H. Drabinsky, Toronto
Karen Dushinski, Edmonton
Kenneth Dushinski, Lakewood, Colorado
Richard and Catherine Fraser
Mira Godard and Reg Bennett
Roy Lacaud Heenan
Dr. Eunice Janzen, Saskatoon
Norman and Dixie Jewison
David and Marie Kaufman
Louise and Bernard Lamarre
Laurentian University Museum and Art Centre,
  Sudbury, Ontario
A. E. MacLennan
Joseph and Zhenia Maslany, Regina
Mendel Art Gallery, Saskatoon
Mira Godard Gallery, Toronto
The National Gallery of Canada, Ottawa
Margaret R. Odishaw
Gerald N. Pencer
Dr. and Mrs. Zelick Perler
Ann and Roger Phillips, Regina
Ken and Karen Powell
Bob and Lasha Roche
Charles Russell, Edmonton
Carol and J. R. Shaw
Susan Whitney Gallery, Regina
Veronica and David Thauberger
Trépanier Baer Gallery, Calgary
Terry and Michele Veeman
Winnipeg Art Gallery

as well as the artist and those lenders who prefer to remain anonymous.

List of Exhibited Works

Albert and Victoria 1988, cat. 43, p. 67

Albrecht 1990, cat. 66, p. 82

Altamira I 1991, cat. 53, p. 73

Andrea I 1993, cat. 90, p. 103

Arthur 1988, cat. 42, p. 66

Arti 1994, cat. 75, p. 88

Asleep in His Mother's House 1988, cat. 28, p. 55

Assyrian Cows 1987, cat. 40, p. 65

Auguste 1993, cat. 24, p. 53

Ayrshire 1993, cat. 60, p. 79

Ayrshire 1993, cat. 61, p. 79

Beverly I 1993, cat. 92, p. 103

Bosseur 1991, cat. 57, p. 77

Boxer Table 1986, cat. 78, p. 93

Bull Moose 1989, cat. 83, p. 97

Calf Table 1986, cat. 77, p. 93

Celtic Horse Table 1996, cat. 88, p. 100

Cézanne 1981, cat. 13, p. 45

Cézanne I 1986, cat. 14, p. 47

Cézanne I 1986, cat. 15, p. 47

Cézanne II 1986, cat. 16, p. 47

Cézanne II 1986, cat. 17, p. 49

Cézanne III 1986, cat. 18, p. 49

Cheyanne 1994, cat. 72, p. 87

Chicoute 1994, cat. 62, p. 80

Chloé 1994, cat. 68, p. 84

Chloé II 1994, cat. 100, p. 105

Clarence II 1995, cat. 108, p. 106

Clarisse I 1993, cat. 91, p. 103

Cortez 1988/1991, cat. 31, p. 57

Dear Vincent 1983, cat. 1, p. 35

Dear Vincent 1983/1984, cat. 2, p. 35

Dear Vincent 1983/1986, cat. 3, p. 35

Dorothy I 1993, cat. 93, p. 103

Le Douanier 1989, cat. 23, p. 52

Elinore 1989, cat. 48, p. 71

Elka II 1995, cat. 107, p. 106

Enid I 1993, cat. 94, p. 103

Escher's Cow I 1993, cat. 95, p. 104

Escher's Cow III 1993, cat. 89, p. 102

The Evil Moon Guides the Santa Maria to the New World 1990, cat. 33, p. 58

Explorer Table 1991, cat. 86, p. 99

Foreshortened Standing Cow 1985/1986, cat. 35, p. 62

Fox Table 1991, cat. 85, p. 98

Géricault 1990, cat. 49, p. 71

Girt 1988, cat. 64, p. 82

Gris 1991, cat. 54, p. 74

Guddi 1994, cat. 74, p. 88

Hamish 1994/1995, cat. 76, p. 90

The Inventor on His Invention 1988, cat. 29, p. 55

Joan of Arc 1990, cat. 32, p. 57

Jori 1994, cat. 69, p. 86

June II 1994, cat. 104, p. 106

Justin I 1994, cat. 103, p. 105

Kiran 1994, cat. 70, p. 86

Lascaux 1988, cat. 41, p. 66

Luke I 1994, cat. 101, p. 105

Manfighter 1986, cat. 37, p. 63

Manitoba 1988, cat. 27, p. 54

Mat I 1994, cat. 102, p. 105

Meena 1994, cat. 73, p. 89

Minuet Minuit 1988, cat. 82, p. 96

Monet 1993, cat. 26, p. 52

Morris 1987, cat. 79, p. 94

Morris and Eve 1988/1995, cat. 81, p. 94

Morris Sonorous 1988, cat. 80, p. 94

My Picasso 1981, cat. 19, p. 50

The Opening 1988, cat. 22, p. 51

The Painter 1986, cat. 11, p. 44

The Pasture 1984-1985, cat. 34, pp. 59-61

Le petit danseur 1988, cat. 20, p. 50

Potter 1990, cat. 50, p. 72

Potter II 1995, cat. 105, p. 106

Princess Louise 1988/1989, cat. 44, p. 68

Régine 1986, cat. 36, p. 63

Reindeer Table 1991/1995, cat. 84, p. 97

Rendez-vous II 1992, cat. 87, p. 99

Renoir 1993, cat. 25, p. 53

Rudy II 1995, cat. 106, p. 106

Sam I 1993, cat. 96, p. 104

Sandhya 1994, cat. 71, p. 87

Sasha I 1994, cat. 99, p. 105

Smoothly She Shifted 1986/1987, cat. 39, p. 64

Snow 1989, cat. 47, p. 70

Sonny Samson I 1993, cat. 98, p. 104

Son of Samson 1993, cat. 97, p. 104

Standing Pablo 1988, cat. 21, p. 51

Taureau 1986, cat. 38, p. 63

Teevo 1993, cat. 59, p. 78

Teevo's Mom 1991-1992, cat. 58, p. 78

The Terrorized 1988, cat. 30, p. 56

Too-in-Wan 1994, cat. 67, p. 84

Topiary 1991, cat. 52, p. 74

Uccello 1989, cat. 65, p. 83

Valadon 1990, cat. 51, p. 72

Vie en Vie 1991, cat. 55, p. 76

Vie en Vie I 1991, cat. 56, p. 76

Vincent 1982, cat. 5, p. 37

Vincent 1982/1986, cat. 6, p. 39

Vincent (Japanese) 1982, cat. 9, p. 43

Vincent No. 4 1982, cat. 4, p. 37

Vincent Self-portrait Series 1982-1983/1987, cat. 8, p. 41

Vincent Ultimo 1982/1994, cat. 10, p. 43

Vuillard 1989, cat. 45, p. 69

Vuillard 1989/1995, cat. 46, p. 69

Walking the Dark Side 1987/1991, cat. 12, p. 45

Wounded Vincent 1982/1994, cat. 7, p. 38

Zeta 1995, cat. 63, p. 80

Photo Credits

The Montreal Museum of Fine Arts wishes to thank the owners and custodians of the works illustrated for providing photographic material for reproduction.

Photographs were taken by:

Art and Architecture Photography, Victoria, British Columbia, cat. 41

Douglas Udell Gallery, cats. 2, 16, 28, 38, 59, 61, 67, 76, 89

Don Hall, cats. 1, 5, 7, 14, 17, 19, 21, 30, 31, 33, 36, 37, 39, 40, 45-51, 54, 56, 58, 60, 62, 65, 66, 77, 79-82, 84, 90-108

Jim Jardine, cat. 88

Grant Kernen, cats. 6, 74

Laurentian University Museum and Art Centre, Sudbury, Ontario, cat. 83

Ernest Mayer, cat. 27

Mendel Art Gallery, Saskatoon, cat. 4

Mira Godard Gallery, cat. 43

The Montreal Museum of Fine Arts, cat. 8
  Christine Guest, cats. 9, 20, 44, 78
  Brian Merrett, cats. 29, 63

Thomas E. Moore, Toronto, cats. 11, 15, 18, 22, 23, 26, 32, 34, 42, 57

The National Gallery of Canada, cat. 13

Richard Pare, cat. 55

Chris Thomas, cats. 70-73, 75, 87

Rudolf Zwamborn, Lotus Studio, Edmonton, cats. 3, 10, 24, 25, 35, 52, 53, 64, 68, 69, 85, 86